ACCLAIM FOR SHOEMONEY

I was told this is where I am supposed to put all the awesome things that have been said about me like all the press and individuals who have praised me. But instead of including all the acclaim I have received from little places like Google, Microsoft, or Yahoo or bragging about how I have been on the cover of Investor's Business Daily and in pretty much every major publication in the world, I am just going to tell you to trust me.

I am awesome.

Nothing's Changed

BUT

My Change

The ShoeMoney Story

JEREMY R. SCHOEMAKER

WITH KATE SPROUSE

To the women in my life who have made all things possible,
beyond my craziest dreams.

My Wife, Doctor J. Elizabeth Schoemaker

My Daughters, Juliet & Joslyn Schoemaker

My Mom, Joyce Schoemaker

My Sister, Andrea Schoemaker

My Aunt, Carol Becca

My Mother-in-Law, Susan Baron

My Pepper Potts, Anna Zagozda.

My Business Associate, Missy Ward

My friend, Jennifer Slegg

CONTENTS

FOREWORD

I remember the first day I heard about a guy named "ShoeMoney." It was 2006.

I was working as the senior marketing executive at Playboy Enterprises at the time, overseeing their digitally-based business lines including Internet, search/SEO, e-commerce, affiliate marketing, online subscriptions and more. I was at a party at the Playboy Mansion speaking with an associate about the biggest blogs and blog personalities on the web in the context of building out an entire blog network for Playboy, and whether it could work. This guy named "ShoeMoney" came up. My associate asked me if I ever heard of this character or seen his blog. I hadn't.

But I remember thinking, "Who would have the nuts to call himself ShoeMoney?"

Little did I know that years later, I would become very good friends with Jeremy, or "Shoe" as I call him, and that we would both return—together—for several huge parties at the exact place where I first heard of him: the Playboy Mansion. Oh, the irony.

In 2007, I left Playboy for greener career pastures. Yes, even as a single, young 30's, straight guy, there ARE greener pastures. I joined Azoogle (which eventually became Epic Advertising/Epic Media Group) as Chief Marketing Officer.

In my very first week, the first person that people at the company told me I HAD to meet was ShoeMoney.

I said, "I've heard of him."

What I didn't know were the details of his past. Super-affiliate. Blogger extraordinaire. Conference organizer. Speaker. Creative marketing guy.

An unabashedly successful millionaire. That ShoeMoney logo. The huge check from Google, which is still an Internet sensation today.

I sent him an email, and we set up a phone call to get to know each other. I remember asking him, "Where are you based? Where do you live?"

When he responded, "Nebraska," I said, "Wait. Where???"

It's just not someplace you immediately think an Internet and technology genius (don't worry, buddy, I won't use the word "guru") would live. I thought he was living on one of the coasts because I just assumed that the most talented minds in the industry all had to live either East or West, you know, near an actual body of water that's a little bigger than Capital Beach Lake.

Silly me. Knowing what I know now, I should have expected Shoe would be close neighbors with Warren Buffet.

Little did I know years later, I would—like Shoe—live in the middle of the country near an only slightly bigger body of water. I'm a 1-hour flight away from him and we've forged a tight relationship and business partnership. I spend time with his family, at his house, and then they come back and visit us.

The deal we have is that every time he's on my home turf in Chicago, I pay for meals and, *ahem*, entertainment. Every time I'm on his home turf, he pays. I still say he gets the way better end of that deal—which is a surprise to no one—because however much cheaper things are in Chicago compared to New York or Los Angeles, that's how much cheaper it is in Nebraska compared to Chicago. But that's okay, Shoe. I guess I just need to come to Nebraska more.

Obviously, my thoughts and feelings about him are from a business and professional standpoint, as well as a personal one. I mean, we've worked in the same field for a good chunk of each of our lives. That was the basis for our relationship and me getting to know him, his wife, J, and his girls.

But I would be remiss if I didn't mention the personal stuff, because that's more important anyway, and because this book is as much about what makes Shoe tick on a personal level as much as it is about his accolades. I won't steal his thunder by telling any great stories about him. Trust me. On the pages that follow you will get plenty of those and he can tell them better, anyway.

I'm really proud of how we have built our businesses and how we complement each other's thinking from a marketing standpoint. But I can tell you that I'm probably most proud to call him a good friend. You ever have one of those people who you feel like you met or got to know about 5 years too late, but who you know will just be in your life forever? That's him for me. And by the way, we couldn't be more opposite of each other in some (or maybe all) respects.

You will learn all about Shoc when you read this book. You will—truly—learn things about him that he's never told you on his blog or even in a drunken stupor one night in Vegas or at the Playboy Mansion. The stories and experiences he tells are fascinating and I can say that I would never have done a fraction of the things he had the balls to do. I'm just not wired that way, perhaps many of you aren't either. Heck, I think most people aren't wired that way. And that's why he's such a fascinating guy, and why most people are inherently drawn to him.

Yet, oddly, his experiences are ones that are relatable to anyone. Shoe was teased as a kid for his weight; even if you were never overweight, you were once a kid and as kids we were all teased, at least a little—ya' know, acne or facial hair or braces or glasses. We all remember how that felt and how it sticks with us to this day.

Shoe was scraping for money early in his professional life, well before he had his own logo in his backyard pool. We have ALL had money problems at one point or another and can relate to "scraping."

Shoe had a series of what one might consider "odd jobs" to make ends meet, all of which ultimately helped him figure out what he did (and maybe more importantly, did not) want to do. Heck, I sold porcelain collector plates in my first job—what did you do? Many of us can relate to the fact that the road you go down initially is not the same one you end up on years later. Lots of twists and turns, and wrong exits, but you find the right road because of all the wrong turns. Just like Shoe did.

He had several run-ins with law enforcement while trying to beat the system. When haven't any of us been irresponsible or done something really stupid, or even pushed the limits of what you can get away with? We all have, to varying degrees. Maybe we didn't spend a night in jail for it, but we can still relate.

His stories and experiences are relatable on the surface, but the substance of Shoe's experiences is one-of-a-kind Shoe. I suppose that's because he's truly a one-of-a-kind guy, and why he will always be the most interesting, fascinating and compelling person—and friend—I will ever hope to know.

I was really touched that he asked me to write this Foreword. Why? Well, for starters, I know a shit-ton of people are going to read this book and he could have asked one of about a hundred people. I don't claim to know a whole lot about the exact reasons WHY some books and memoirs are more compelling than others; I just know that this is one of them.

A lot has changed with Shoe over the years. His "change" has changed, that is for sure. But one thing that I don't think will ever change is his regard for people and how important his circle of friends and partners are to him. Please don't mistake this to mean that he won't come after you if you try to screw him over and don't think for a second that his millions of followers won't hear all about you and your crumby little scheme afterward. That "shit list" is not one you really want to be on, let's be honest.

But now I'm getting ahead of myself. Don't worry. He'll get into all that in a few pages.

Strap in for one of the most interesting, fun, emotional reads you'll ever have.

And, Shoe, here's to another couple awesome decades that are rich with stories, experiences and "change." Yes, that kind of change.

— Mike Sprouse

Nothing's Changed but My Change

Author's Note

This is a work of non-fiction.

It's my story from my memory. I thought about changing the real names of the people I mention here but then I was like, fuck it. All the names are true to honor and embarrass the guilty parties.

Special Note: All spelling and grammar errors are intentional. I wrote this book for people, not for grammar-tards.

1
Intros and Angles

I'm not going to tell the story the way it happened.

I'm going to tell it the way I remember it.

- CHARLES DICKENS,

Great Expectations

Of course I'm writing a book.

So much crazy shit has happened in my life sometimes even I don't believe it all. I have been at the bottom of everything and today I'm like the king. It's good to have the perspective from both. Not many people do. And after all, I'm a storyteller. That's probably the first thing I knew I was good at. No one can tell a story like I can. I can make a story about a crock pot exciting, for God's sake. In my life though, I don't have to think too hard to find a good story. I have stories about guns and shake downs and scams. There was the stuff that happened in Florida and the time I had to hide in Ohio. There were those times I *almost* died. And there's happy stuff too. Lots of happy stories and badass exciting stories. I even have a few love stories to tell you.

And so now I'm writing a book, to tell my stories, because I can.

Now you're probably like, "Why the hell should I care about your stories?"

There are lots of answers to that question, idiot.

They're entertaining, for starters. Also, it's good practice to see life through someone else's experiences. You can learn something. I think it's called vicarious, or something. Look--I might not be the best writer. My grammar is crap. I barely got out of high school, but we'll get to that story later. I pay people to do all that stuff for me now BECAUSE I CAN.

I have become successful because I know how to figure things out. That doesn't mean I'm going to give you a six-point plan for you to become successful overnight. That's not going to happen in this book because I'm savvy as shit. And I can't teach you to be savvy as shit in one book. But if you pay attention, I promise that you are going to learn a lot of stuff you can apply to your life, starting with a few helpful hints about happiness. I just want to be clear that this isn't a manual or a text book. Manuals are for pussies.

If you're still not sold, I have (at least) one more reason.

Have you ever bought something online? Well, if you have there's a really good chance that you bought it because of me—directly or indirectly. I'm a marketer. I define marketing as exploiting people's passions for profits. And when I say people, I mean YOU. I have never hidden any of this. I'm a really transparent guy. So here, in my book, you have the chance to be inside the head of a really powerful marketer. That has got to be worth something.

If you know me at all, have ever heard me speak or you follow my blog, then you know my official introduction (or parts of it). I'm one of the most successful Internet marketers of our time. I know how to write copy. I know how to sell. One time a guy actually bought me a brand new BMW to say thanks for the sick amount of product I moved for him. I'm a search-engine optimizer. I killed it before SEO was even a term. I'm a serial entrepreneur. I've conceptualized, built and sold six companies including the mother of YouTube. I had a weekly segment shown during Good Morning America to advise emerging businesses. I'm the guy who was once living off of unemployment and then *suddenly* had a seven-figure income. I'm the guy holding that legendary $132,994.97 Google check. (Seriously. Google, "check" and there's my mug.) I'm the guy with the blog that Technorati consistently ranks in the top 100 blogs. I was established as the most influential person on the Internet by Fast Company in 2010, a ranking (I have to add) in which I beat Shaquille O'Neal and Britney Spears --by a lot. By all accounts of the obvious and published, I'm successful. I have made a lot of money and I wield a crazy amount of influence.

This is me with the check. Did you really need to read the caption?

There are also other accounts of me and my work that have said I'm the guy who games the system; I'm a scam artist, a huckster. I'm the guy who makes money by telling people he makes money but has never legitimately done it. I'm the guy who blurs the lines of ethics, morals, and legality. And I'm always the guy who is "going downhill." People have been saying that since 2003. They call me out as lazy, illiterate, stupid, and worthless and wait for my demise.

There are times when these slams bother me, but then I remember that tens of thousands of people read what I say, every day. And if one in 10,000 people disapprove, well then that still means my approval is ridiculously higher than any president ever has.

Like I said, I'm transparent and as a transparent guy I have never hidden the fact that I see angles. I always have. I always will. I guess that's what you call a gift, when you have something that average people do not. So let's say that my gift is that I have always seen ways to get things done, opportunities to benefit within a flawed system, strategies to solve a problem, means to make money in practically any situation. I see these angles and then I take them - immediately and aggressively. And that is a big reason why I have been successful. Opportunities are everywhere but they never last long. You need to be brave enough to take them when you see them. I am. I do.

That might sound sexy and dangerous. And right now, no doubt, you're imagining me with my ShoeMoney logo proudly stretched across the chest of my t-shirt, soaring through the air like fucking Superman, peeking in from time to time on the crooks at Google and eBay and Facebook and Apple, searching out angles within their schemes. These angles I will find and then heroically bring to the masses—the hard working men and women whose opportunities have been snatched up by villainous corporate schemes. And I certainly don't want to deprive you of this image.

Hell, I don't want to deprive myself of this image.

That ShoeMoney logo across my chest is real, after all. It's a real symbol of what I wanted to become someday in my grown-up world: the rich superhero. I used to sit in school when I was seven or eight, not focused on a single thing my teachers were saying, drawing ninjas in death duels with these awesome swords and bows, fighting to the destruction of everything. And then, I would imagine that I would drop into the death duel to smash in the ninja's faces and save the day (and the hot chick with the big tits in the oriental get-up). In that world I wasn't fat, geeky, lazy Jeremy. I was something more than my person. I had a persona.

The Green Lantern has always been my all-time favorite super hero. He was a guy that was limited by nothing but his imagination. His superpowers came directly from his will and his weakness from his fear. I saw myself in those terms, pushing myself—if only at first in my imagination and in those sketches—to be something more, to be brave and confident, to let go of my fear and be willing to do what I had to.

That's about the same time that I started to sketch my logo. If you haven't seen it by now, it's a shield with a dollar sign in the center. It's not crazy complicated to figure out. Money is at the center of everything. That's what it means. This brings me to my first truth. See, we're not even out of the first chapter and already I'm hammering you with knowledge.

Here's the deal. **Having money isn't everything, but not having it is.**

Take that to the bank.

Now remember, I'm only about eight years old at this time. And in my real little-kid world I have no money, I suck at school and I'm always the crazy, fat kid that starts trouble. So a future in super-heroism wasn't looking all that good for me. But even superheroes have moms. And my mom was an honest-to-God pillar of our community and probably the most beloved English teacher our local high school ever saw. In fact, I remember opening my report card one time and spotting a "D" that I know I didn't earn. It was more like an "F". And do you want to know what my report card said next to that letter "D"? The note read, "Your mom is a wonderful person." I swear to God. That was her effect. People frickin' loved her enough to give her son a passing grade he hadn't earned. And she loved me too, despite myself and my downfalls.

Fast forward a few years and now I'm fifteen. At this point, I am still broke, still sucking at school and now, the even crazier fat kid. My mom decided she needed to help me out. So what does she do? She helps me land a job.

At this time, she had no idea she was delivering me to the birthplace of my own alter-ego.

That's right. Of all places, my mom scored me a job at this pizza joint called Happy Joe's. When I first started there, they rotated me between all the various tasks. I did everything from running the cash register and doing the dishes to making the pizzas and slicing them up. The management saw right away that I had a God-given talent for cutting the pizzas. The normal dipshit cuts a pizza in half, vertically, then in half, horizontally, then each of those fourths in half again until they get perfectly proportional slices. But, like I said, I had an honest to God talent in that I could yield the 15-inch machete-like blade and fly counter-clockwise with the same-result. It took me a fraction of the time of my pizza making predecessors. I didn't have to stop and think and proportion that shit, I just did it right there on the cut table.

With my skills, there were no longer a slew of pizzas in a bottle neck waiting to be cut. I was slicing them up as soon as they came out of the oven. Back in the kitchen we always listened to rap music. It was a combination of that and my ninja pizza-cutting skills that one day, my co-worker Nick Van Acker turned to me and said, "What's up ShoeMoney on the cut?" From then on that was what I was called— "ShoeMoney." They even made me a triple XL tee shirt that said "ShoeMoney" on the front and "On the Cut" on the back.

That's how ShoeMoney was a born—a persona for a crazy fat kid who could really cut a pizza and had never been cool before.

Basically, that was the height of my fame and glamour—for a while.

The other thing about me, that you need to know, is that I am always willing to do what others are not. Yes, I see angles and opportunities and in many ways and times I have been really lucky and fortunate. But I have also been willing to put the work in, to take a risk, to push the boundaries in order to see something through. So much of my professional success is due to this—100%. I tell people all of the time exactly what to do to make money and more often than not, these people will find an excuse not to do what they could. I don't make excuses. I do it. I am always willing to do what others are willing not to do. It has nothing to do with luck or glamour or good and evil. It has everything to do with **willingness.**

This relentless will that I operate under has made all the difference in my life. It has been the source of all my success and happiness. But there is one space in my life in which it has also been my biggest flaw.

There is not a single memory I have from the first 25 years of my life where I was not fat. Seriously, I was just always fat. My whole family was fat. And when you're fat—like really, truly fat and obese—you live with a different quality of life. As a kid I used to scheme up all sorts of ways to get out of gym class so I wouldn't have to be naked in front of anyone or have to move around and run. It was just embarrassing and uncomfortable, sweaty and itchy. And I never had a girlfriend. Sure, I was infatuated with many girls but my insecurities prevented me from pulling the trigger. I knew that I couldn't be *that guy* in real life. I wasn't going to get the girl. And so I also got used to the idea that I would never get married and that I would never have kids or become a father. I was willing to accept all of that. I had accepted all of that. I had even accepted…no—scratch that. It was more than acceptance. It was expectation. I fully expected that I wouldn't live to see my thirtieth birthday.

Ironically, that acceptance probably fueled and fanned my willingness for everything else in my life. I learned how to be extroverted, even when I was embarrassed. I became brave as only the biggest guy in the room knows he has to be. I took chances that only a guy who doesn't expect to be here for very long takes. I never felt like I had to prove my choices to anyone. I did what I wanted. And in many ways that served me well. I learned what I was good at, what I liked, and who I was without excuses. But no one can really live a full life and thrive without hope. My expectations for a short and lonely life should have been enough to kill me.

That could have been the entire story, not just the beginning. Jeremy was the guy who was really fat and fucked around a lot and had a bunch of crazy stories until he died one night in his sleep. That could have been my story, just like my friend, Bryce. But it wasn't. Somewhere along my path I course corrected, or maybe I have to say that my course was corrected for me. It's kind of like that movie, *The Adjustment Bureau.*

ADD Side Note: Adjustment Bureau is a cool movie. I definitely recommend that you check that out.

A note about the ADD Side Note: I have a thing, or maybe you want to call it a "problem" with focusing. This isn't the last time you're going to see a side note or a tangent or just a completely disconnected thought out of nowhere. Also, I'll probably change what I call them. Just so you know. That's how my brain works and that's how I tell a story. Buckle up and deal.

However I explain it, my life changed and I didn't end up like Bryce. I lived into my thirties with a lot of good fortune. And I will admit that sometimes I got lucky. A beautiful and fiercely intelligent woman fell in love with me. I realized that I could do what I was naturally good at and turn that into my real, grown-up job. I saw that job grow into a brand, a full company, and a lot of money. I learned how to be confident every day, despite the odds, and I learned to really believe in myself and my ideas.

I have to tell you another thing here. There are lots of times that I did get "lucky," like I was saying. I was in the right place at the right time or something like that. But I want to be clear from the beginning that you can't bet on luck. You can only bet on yourself and what you can control. So focus on that and stop playing the lottery.

Everybody struggles. I started to tell you before that I barely graduated high school at all. I failed English two years in a row. I mean straight out failed, like had to do it again. I eventually survived high school and went on to college, but with zero intention of getting a degree. In fact, I should probably admit to you now before you get any further invested into my story that I have never even read a single book, cover to cover.(Hey I've listened to audio books, but never actually read one.) But like I've told you before, I see angles and I'm always willing to do what others are willing not to do. And right now I see an angle—a reason—to write a book and I'm willing to do it, to put it all out there.

My stories are sad and crazy and funny. But mostly they are hopeful. They are all about the pursuit of happiness, a pursuit in which I have been successful against a lot of odds. And that is what I want to share.

So I'm writing a book because I want to tell you that story with all its crazy shorter stories like only I remember it.

2
I Am God

Trust no one.

- *THE X FILES*

What a crafty and jaded way to get your attention. I admit that. And it's ironic because I just told you that the point of this whole story is hope. I've already blown the ending. I win because I'm awesome. Today I live with my family and we're so happy there's a frickin' rainbow over our house. That should tell you, at least, that I believe that happiness and hope have a lot to do with relationships.

I do.

So you're probably expecting this part of the story to be about how I learned to trust.

It isn't.

I don't.

These next stories are about why I don't trust anyone and how that's a good and responsible way to be.

It's a funny thing, this process of explaining how you've come to be the way you are and why you believe the things you believe. You have to trace a complicated series of events backwards to find the first domino that fell and began a certain direction. And as I've done this I keep getting back to the same place, where I didn't really want to go. But since I can't seem to find another honest starting point, I'll go to the obvious.

I don't trust anyone because—thankfully—I first learned to not trust God.

Believing in Him as a kid really screwed up my perspective on life. Now, by no means am I picking a religious debate with you here. Maybe if we were having a beer or shooting pool we would debate the hypocrisy of the church and the manipulation of religion. I would love that. But this isn't a discussion. This is my book. And since I have the undisputed stage here, pay fucking attention. I am not talking about religion or the church or any sanctioned or historical way of seeing God. I am not making any statements about the existence and realities of God. I am not trying to convince you into any one way of believing. Quite simply, I am saying that the way I learned to believe in God screwed up the way I handled my life.

I left a lot of shit up to that guy, stuff I should have taken control over and could have affected. But I was taught to believe that everything in my life comes from God and also that God gets credit for everything that happens. As a kid, this gets neatly packaged up into prayer. I learned to pray for what I wanted and say thank you for what I got. It was ingrained into my thinking that this was the simple arrangement. If something I wanted didn't happen, it meant that I didn't pray hard enough. So I prayed harder. And harder. And harder.

Sometimes, like magic, this worked! Every once in a while I managed to pull a "D" on the spelling test I didn't study for. Most times, though, it didn't work so magically. Most times it would end in frickin' disaster—another failed test, another big fat "F". And still every night I would get back on my knees, next to my bed, with my eyes squeezed as tight as they could possibly be squeezed and my lips mushed together with all my effort, trying to push out a good prayer like a shit—as hard as humanly possible.

I didn't give a whole lot of thought to this arrangement because it suited me. Granted it wasn't successful. But it suited me. It gave me a convenient excuse for what did and did not happen in my life. If I got an "F" on my spelling test it wasn't because I spent the night screwing around and not studying; it was because I didn't pray enough. And if I did push out my prayers as hard as shit and still I didn't get what I wanted, well then, I settled on the understanding that God knew what I deserved.

Trusting God like that taught me to believe two things early in life. The first thing I learned was that I wasn't in control of my life and therefore not responsible for the shit that happened in it. Second of all, I learned that I wasn't worthy of a whole lot of good stuff, because the grades, the gym class reprieves, Tom Cruise's mojo, and the black Porsche 911 Turbo convertible of my prayers never magically showed up. That stunted sense of responsibility and lack of self-worth got stuck way down inside me. It's still there, I think, because sometimes I feel it like a whiney rag in my ass.

The difference is that I see it now, and I have since stopped wishing and praying and hoping for the things that make me happy. Instead, I work for them and earn them and then enjoy the shit out of them. I will never trust anyone, even a deity, to do that work for me ever again.

Fast forward to the first conference I ever attended was in San Jose. Here is where I met this hilarious SEO guy who loved my blog and presented me with a God of Money statue. I forget his name but his online moniker was Hawaii SEO. I really appreciated that gesture so I gave him a ShoeMoney tee shirt in what I thought was an awesome exchange, since I didn't expect much from the good luck and blessing from any driftwood. It's been on my desk ever since and my revenues are up, so I have decided to just let that little guy be while I continue to do my thing and enjoy my nightly commutes on the Ducati Monster 696 which, by the way, is better than anything I ever fucking dreamed up in my prayers as a kid.

Side Note: While I'm not much of a religious participant, to say the least, I do have to say that growing up in a Lutheran church taught me one thing. **Martin Luther was a fucking badass who was willing to risk everything for what he believed in.** I was going to explain a little about Martin Luther here but then I thought if a religious derelict like me knows who he is then I'm assuming you do to. Except, I guess, if you're Catholic and if that's the case well then not picking up this reference is the least of your problems.

My dad has always been critical of the church. From as far back as I can remember he would laugh at the people who attributed their success to a higher power. People always want a one-sided God who gives them what they want. He would point out that there's the other side, as well. For people who thank God for a victory, it also means they're thanking God for someone else's loss, pain and suffering. I always thought my dad was super wise for recognizing this hypocrisy.

Which brings us, officially, to the part where I talk about my dad.

Me and My Dad. Thank God for the caption, again.

And I'll be honest—I'm conflicted about how this is going to come out.

My dad is a man with an incredible amount of will—like cheat death four times, build your own company twice, dig out your own fishing pond because you want one in your backyard and then tromp off to Montana to hunt, no-joke, 500-pound elk with his .306 rifle for fun, type of will. He never waited for anything to happen to him; he never consulted God or wife or colleague or son. He just went out and did it. I admire that.

That type of will is a force that can't be reckoned with and beats within someone who doesn't stay in any one place long enough to build anything lasting. Not long ago he was in Spain and nearly broke a fishing world record for weight with a 104 pound catfish catch. The footage is somewhere on YouTube. When he told me about it I thought, "W*ow! What a prize! What a thing to brag about!*" And I think that's what most people would think, don't you?

Well, my dad is the exact opposite of the average person. He really doesn't care about the prize. He is fully immersed in living. He's a hunter, a fisherman, a union worker with dirt under his finger nails and a pickup truck in the yard. It sounds admirably middleclass American and so un-materialistic when I put it like that. But the opposite side of the coin is that when you're building a business or a family, you absolutely have to give a whole lot of shit about the end product just as much, if not ten times more, as you do about the process. If you don't, it's too easy to walk away from the process when it gets hard or boring one day, as it always will and does.

I wasn't trying to be poetic when I said that my dad has cheated death, at least twice. He was a lifelong smoker—started when he was 17. Considering that and how hard he worked, he was actually in pretty good health. Then, at 52 he had a stroke and a heart attack. These turned out to be symptoms of viral cardiomyopathy, which can happen to anyone, really—smoker or not. In my dad's case, the virus was bad luck, exacerbated by his lifestyle. The doctors told him that he could be a candidate for a heart transplant, but given his background, the odds weren't good. So they gave him 6 months to live, a mechanical stand-in heart, and a prayer. He consented, but I'm fairly fucking certain he didn't pray. He just decided there was no way in hell he was going to die, I guess, and a donor heart came along for a full transplant. Today transplants aren't the same. Today it's like fixing a carburetor where you fit a piece here and there and fuse it together and jump it. Back then he got a full frickin' new heart through a series of dangerous, high-risk procedures.

Again, the doctors gave him shitty odds and in one procedure he actually croaked. He literally flat-lined and died on the operating table. He was gone for a full two minutes, but evidently one of the residents that night (who was equally strong willed), got on top of my dad and started double axing on his chest. He broke three of his ribs in the process, but eventually restarted his heart. Today he's still ticking as one of the oldest living heart transplant recipients on the planet. His doctors tell him to take it easy and that his odds to keep living like he does are shitty. He smiles at them and then splits for Spain to catch a massive catfish.

I do admire that will. He's got the *"I'll-do-whatever-the-fuck-I-want-to"* will. And he saw angles, like I do. I guess I get that from him. Also he pushed boundaries, just like I do. We are both *get-your-hands-dirty-if-that's-how-the-job-gets-done* kind of guys.

His long-term job based my family in Moline, IL. I'm not surprised if you haven't heard of it. It's one of the four cities that make up the Quad-Cities, a relatively unheard of area that is credited mostly as the largest metropolitan area between Chicago, Omaha, Minneapolis, St. Louis, and Kansas City. So basically, Moline is part of a place that is best known as a not-place. (I think I read that on Wikipedia. It's frickin' hilarious.) But for the purposes of my story and the stories of thousands of Midwestern farm implement industry workers, Moline is a place that matters a whole hell of a lot. At the height of economic and agricultural prosperity, the home factories for John Deere, Alcoa, Caterpillar, Case, and International Harvester were all in Moline.

My father worked at International Harvester's Farmall factory ever since he was 18. My memories of him are going in as a maintenance welder on 9-5 shifts, with the occasional second shift. Because he was a maintenance welder he wasn't really needed until something would break. When he told stories he would talk about kicking back between jobs—sleeping, on occasion, in a random truck or back office. But for ten years before that he was working his way up as a production welder who was paid by the number of parts he produced. He came home, long after my mom had put my sister and me to bed, with holes in his shirts and pants from the weld spotter and open sores on his feet caused by weld that had trickled into his boots while he stood still for long hours welding.

He worked hard for a long time, but by the time I was old enough to really remember him on the job, he had worked his way up as someone who sort of mattered. He had put in his time and he was in the union. He also had a lot of friends and with those friends came connections. All together this gave him a perspective to see angles.

In the Midwest the 1980s were known as the Rust Belt Days because so many farming implement plants closed down. Everywhere you went jobs were dried up and old factories were rusted out. If your town was really lucky a mega company like John Deere or Case was able to keep things going, sometimes by acquiring other failing companies. That's pretty much what happened in Moline when Case acquired the International Harvester plant. But it wasn't a clean win-win. Tons of guys still lost their jobs and Case inherited a major headache: thousands of parts they couldn't use.

My dad's idea was to streamline all the replacement parts for Case and International Harvester products alike so they could be machined out, compatible and integratable for every tractor on the production line. With two partners he started a viable company called Admiral Improvement, which took contracts with both Case and John Deere to execute dad's modern industrial idea. It was great for the companies. It was great for the laid-off guys who were re-hired. It was great for business. He was on the front page of the Wall Street Journal as a success story. He was interviewed by NHK out of Japan (think Newsweek) as proof that the American entrepreneurial spirit was alive and well despite the rampant plant closures of the Rust Belt Days.

But this didn't mean a whole lot to my dad. Honestly, I think he built the damn company—not because he wanted to be wealthy and successful as an entrepreneur or even because he enjoyed his craft— but to hook up all his buddies. And that's exactly what he did. My mom always said that he was constantly being the hero to people who didn't care. I'm not sure if you call it heroism or cronyism, but he certainly did hook up his friends, which ultimately led to the downfall of his company. It started with him being the bigger man—going without a paycheck for stretches as long as eleven weeks so that he could make payroll for his guys. But the sacrifices went beyond surviving on my mom's teacher salary. He made them partners and executives and they became alcoholics and embezzlers.

That's how I saw it.

Scandal, mistakes, and extortion aside, my dad also had this fully operational machinery and paint facility on his hands while Admiral Improvement sludged along in its contracts for a number of years. And just because he wanted to (and because he could) he started making different kinds of fishing lures for his weekend fishing trips. That was the inception of his second successful business. After several prototypes and tests, he eventually perfected a new lure that mimicked a crippled alewife (a type of herring). He used it and liked it so he figured that other fishermen would too. He sent out boxes of his crippled alewives to commercial fishermen and began to drum up a client base.

To make a very long and depressing story short, after conceiving and building these two wildly successful businesses, cheating death with first a mechanical and then a transplanted heart and awakening from a full cardiac arrest, my dad returned to life as a union worker at International Harvester to get his pension and continue to earn overtime because he had nothing else left. His buddies and Admiral Improvement ate him alive. No longer in the position to manufacture his fishing lures, the company was eventually sold to one of the largest fishing lure manufactures in the world. The design is still one of their top grossing products each year.

The whole thing left me totally baffled and in many ways abandoned as a kid who was looking—as all kids do—for guidance and inspiration. I guess that's where I'm conflicted. Because, you see, I learned a hell of a lot from my dad. He taught me to never leave anything up to chance. I saw that there were no safety nets. I learned that you can't really trust anyone. In fact, that's the biggest lesson if I had to pick just one. I heard my dad say that God was all BS and to never trust anyone. But still he had a soft spot in his heart and he couldn't help himself from putting a lot of faith in other people. And every single time that he did they fucked him over royally.

That's a brutal thing to learn at a young age. But I guess it's really a brutal lesson to learn at any age.

I want to be happy and blessed. I want success and wealth. I want what I earn. I work and sweat really hard for it and I'll give a lot of it to you for free of my own will. I will gladly tell you everything that I have ever learned, cure your addiction to the promise of magic pills, send you a box filled with the new prototypes I'm working on, and I won't charge you a dime or lose a wink of sleep. (Don't worry about me, there's a method to that madness which in no way cuts into my profit margins.

More on that later.) But I won't trust you. I will never trust anyone for my life, my work and my happiness.

I guess that's the take-away from all the complication and psychology here. My life is on me. It's not on my dad. It's not on God. It's not on the last guy who tried to screw me over.

I can't tell you how much simpler your life will become if you can actually hold yourself responsible instead of some deity.

Then you too can be your own God.

3
I Used to Be Fat

Ladies, my Mercedes

Hold fo' in the back,

Two if you fat.

     -NOTORIOUS B.I.G.

Did I mention that I used to be fat?

If you have ever been so fat that your scale has had to twirl around 1 and a half times to "guess" your weight and your skin chafes and stinks between your fat rolls then you already understand everything I'm about to say. And if you haven't ever been so fat that you have a hard time getting the damn deodorant stick up and into your armpits, well then I sort of want to say, "Fuck! You!" and punch you in the face, stringbean.

Not because you're not fat, but because you don't understand.

A few months ago I was flying and I settled my now skinny self into my 12C aisle seat. A woman was already seated in the window seat. I smiled at her and said hello. Other than being middle aged I can't remember a thing about her appearance (which is fine as her only purpose here is to be the standard white skinny thinking bitch). She smiled back and said hello as she continued to eye each passenger walking onto the plane and near our row. Then she leaned over to me, which I totally wasn't expecting, and then said under her breath, "I really hope none of those fat people are sitting between us. It's disgusting. They should have to buy two seats."

I'm never at a loss for words, but I couldn't think of a thing to say to her before she went back to reading her *Good Housekeeping* or whatever.

I've been saying for a while now that in this country that fat people get treated like second-class citizens. But sitting next to this uppity bitch whose panties are in a knot at the thought of brushing arms with a fatty makes me rethink. Being fat puts you in a whole new category of low below everyone else. Being fat means you're a fat-class citizen.

When you're fat, that's all people see. When I was fat, I knew that people didn't look at me and think, *"Oh hey, there's Jeremy. Jeremy's so interesting and sweet and funny."* They looked at me and saw fat. I knew that when people met me for the first time they weren't worried about making a good impression on me. They weren't busy wondering what type of guy I'd turn out to be. They shook my hand and met a fat guy. And when my friends described me, they weren't stuck looking for adjectives. They never said, "Yeah, you know Jeremy—he has brown hair and glasses and he sits behind you in homeroom." All they had to say was, "Jeremy's the really fucking fat kid."

When you are as fat as I was nothing matters more than the fact that you're really fucking fat. And when no one else sees anything more than that, unfortunately you stop seeing anything more than that, too.

I can't separate my childhood from all the ridicule and humiliation that was in it. By the time I was fifteen, I was more than 300 pounds. I weighed more than the V8 305 engine in my friend's Chevy truck. Of course that fun fact was pointed out to me, you know, as a *"joke."* *Hilarious.* And my most frequent nickname was not ShoeMoney. It was *Jabba,* as in *Jabba the Hut.* When I walked somewhere—like from the lunch line to a table—kids would make noises by stomping their feet on the floor and pound their fists on the wheeled-in-tables. It was supposed to sound like the ground was shaking beneath me. Again, *hilarious*. I got the fat Albert "Hey, Hey, Hey!" thing a lot, too. And whenever I ate ANYTHING, I got stares and comments from everyone. If a skinny kid ate a plate of fries, no one noticed. If he ate two (right before gym class) he was only that much cooler. But there is a completely opposite response when fat people eat, regardless of what it is. If I ate a damn apple I got an eye roll and a "Good luck with that!" from the token junior high hot girl. When I ate a slice of pizza I got a disgusted, "No wonder..." from whoever happened to be passing by.

There is nothing harder than being the butt of the joke all of the time. You NEVER get used to the kind of cruelty.

The really awful thing is that it wasn't just the kids. I got it from my teachers, too.

I'm serious.

Yes I was fat—fat as in the *chairs-were-scared-of-me-sitting-on-them*. But I expected a little more discretion, or at least some intelligence, from the adults who were educating me. As it turned out though, they couldn't see beyond the fat either. I mean, my god, I was already horrifically aware of my fat at every waking moment and then each and every year my teachers would point it out as my problem. I couldn't work hard enough because I was fat (and lazy). I couldn't work fast enough because I was fat (and slow). I couldn't read well enough because I was fat (and dumb). Look, I'll frickin' admit that maybe, sometimes, there was some truth that I acted lazy or slow or like a dumb ass. But it wasn't as simple as that. Every kid is a complicated mess of insecurities and raw emotions and fresh brain farts and that's what makes them so fucking adorable.

I never felt adorable. I was just fat. And because I was fat, I was lazy and slow and dumb and less valuable and too big to be fragile.

I don't know how much it helped our physical education, but bowling was actually a unit we had in gym class. It was one I actually liked—no running, no sweat in my back fat, no need to change and be naked in front of anyone else in the locker room. Bowling was a reprieve from all that and a chance to leave school grounds for an hour, a short bus ride away from Hell. It was fun, actually, until the day I forgot to take off my bowling shoes. I was already on the bus, slouched down in my own seat, three rows from the back when Mr. Clark stepped onto the bus. He held up a pair of shoes and I realized immediately that I'd just forgotten about the shoe thing. I never changed back.

It didn't have to be a thing at all but Mr. Clark was an evil asshole. When I got to the front of the bus he handed me my shoes and said, "Oh. Of course. The fat kid who can't see his feet." I can still hear his limp dick voice and those exact words—SO MEAN—and then the laughter all around me as the bus shifted into gear. I never accidentally showed up naked to the first day of school or pissed my pants in public or got caught jerking off under a blanket or into a cherry pie. But if you put all those experiences together and wrapped them up into one surge of embarrassment that was broadcast live across the Internet, I don't think it could be any more horrifying than standing in the front of that bus, trying to get a look at my feet, still in the bowling shoes, while everyone laughed.

Thank you, Mr. Clark. ASSHOLE.

And then there was the cardboard box.

I wasn't lazy or slow or dumb, but I am pretty sure that I was ADD or ADHD or however they diagnose it these days. I just could not focus. The best way I can describe my brain (and it still functions like this) is like an endless web-surfing worm hole. I can't ever seem to get through a full thought before there's a new idea to click and then another and another and another to click through and I can't ever seem to remember where I started. Not surprisingly, this is probably a big reason why the Internet and I get along so well. We work the same way. But that's a whole 'nother chapter for later.

Back to where I was.

…I am pretty sure that I had ADD or ADHD because I have never been able to focus, as I was telling you. But neither of those terms was ever applied to me and none of my teachers ever connected the dots between my lack of focus and my lack of success. But in my fifth grade year it drove Miss Jasiota absolutely nuts. I guess she couldn't concentrate because I couldn't concentrate for more than ten seconds. After several weeks of yelling at me to pay attention to the chalkboard, stay in my seat and to stop drawing ninja turtles in death duels with nunchucks and grenades, Ms. Jasiota invented a wildly progressive educational tool: a cardboard box the size of a refrigerator. One day I walked into class and there it was. There was a six by six inch hole cut out as a window in the front and my desk and chair were inside it. That was my cell and for the next month that's where I was forced to sit and "focus" and learn.

How the hell that strategy of first rate education went on for a month, I can't say, but it did. If you remember, though, my mom was a teacher and a pillar of the community and all that, so at some point she found out about this strategy and went frickin' bat shit. I don't know exactly what she did or who she reamed, but she did something in the realm of bat shit crazy. And after that I didn't have to sit in the cardboard box any more.

I wonder if you feel bad for me yet. And if you are fat, I wonder if you're feeling bad about yourself—or for yourself, yet. But if you aren't fat, I wonder if you feel at all bad about what you have done or said or even thought about the fat people in your life. One of them might even be sitting next to you on your next flight. You never know.

You want to be polite and PC and all that, I'm sure. But I know that there is one question that you're dying to ask me so that you know just how much sympathy I deserve. I will put it out there for you so you don't have to ask.

How the hell did I get so fat?

The truthful answer is simple, as truths tend to be.

I got fat because I ate a lot.

Nutri-system, Jenny Craig, Weight Watchers…a list of magic bullet fat fixes could go on for a good portion of the rest of this book. There are a lot of them. In the United States weight loss is a multi-billion dollar industry because, I believe, Americans don't really want the simple truth. We want things to be mysterious and confusing and out of our control. That way we don't have to take responsibility for ourselves or in this case, for our fat.

I'm not alone in this.

I come from a huge family, and I don't mean that I have a lot of frickin' cousins in the Ozarks. I mean that everyone in my family was fat. But I don't believe in genetics as the fat factor. I would never say I was fat because I was genetically fated to be fat. That's a cop out. My family and I were fat because of the way that we lived. I remember very clearly sitting at my grandma's dinner table with a mound of food on my plate, shoveling down forkfuls at a time. I did not leave the table until my plate was clean. No one did. We were all clean plate clubbers and damn proud of it.

Very quickly, eating became an activity that was totally disconnected from hunger. Food was a thing that had nothing to do with fuel, but it also wasn't really enjoyable. In fact, sometimes it was fucking uncomfortable. Eating meant going until I was gorged on a box of mac and cheese that I made with a full two sticks of butter or mowing down an entire Happy Joe's taco pizza. It was mechanical. There was no halfway. There was eating or not eating. Everything or nothing.

And so I was fat—it was early damage. No one was force feeding me. I wasn't born with any kind of dysfunctional gene resulting in a thyroid disorder or cursed by the magical spell of half-faced Valdemort. So you can stop wondering about how bad you should feel for me. Not even a rat's shit bit. Now we can continue on without that distracting *your* focus.

What you don't realize is that not only should you not feel bad for me, you should envy me. Because beyond all the other stuff, what you really don't understand is that being fat gave me a huge edge. (Pun intended. Give me a break. For high school English flunkies, puns are the stuff "A+" papers must be made of. Oh yea, and this is my book. So suck it.)

There is a universal fat rule. If you are big and you want recognition for anything beyond being just big and fat, everything you do must be even bigger and better than everyone else. If you don't want to be just the fat kid, you have to become the ridiculously hilarious fat kid or the mad genius fat kid or the jacked-up crazy fat kid. You have to do whatever you do as loud possible. At the risk of sounding arrogant here (because I'm usually so modest), I probably could have made a strong run at both the ridiculously hilarious and the mad genius route, but jacked-up crazy also came naturally for me and it was by far the most fun. So instead of being the fat kid who got overlooked, or the sad fat kid showering in the locker room with his shirt on, or always remembered as Fat Jeremy who forgot to take his bowling shoes off and spent a month in a box in Ms. Jasiota's class, I decided to become the crazy fat kid.

If someone jumped into the pool, I had to one up him by doing a cannonball. If someone did a cannonball—well, then I had to do a massive belly flop that splashed the entire pool deck. If my friends were racing motorcycles, I turned it into a jumping contest. And when they jumped 15 feet—well, then I went and got my dad's truck, pulled it up to our bikes, got enough distance for a launch and jumped the whole damn pickup. I one-upped so much I became fearless and because I was fearless I got comfortable pushing the boundaries all the frickin' time. Because I pushed boundaries I learned how to be scrappy and strategic and find my way through the angles with even more confidence.

I really hope I was dropping a fart in this picture.

I'll say it again. When you are big and fat you have to do everything bigger and better, so something besides the humiliating mass of your body gets noticed.

You know that joke about fat chicks? It goes like this:

Why do fat chicks give the best blow jobs?

Because they have to.

People who have been fat all their lives are natural givers. Maybe it's because we don't think we deserve to be loved without having to earn it. I don't know.

When I was in high school I bought a dog for a bitch named Melissa Crouch. I talked about her a lot in the past because I was absolutely obsessed with her as a teenager and she led me along for a few years in a twisted relationship. But in my book she is only going to play a minor role because she's not worth any more than that. At one time I had bought her clothes and make-up and all sorts of other shit too. But the biggest thing I ever bought her was a dog. I fantasized that we would raise the dog together and that is how she would fall in love with me; never mind that I couldn't afford dog food after paying for the thing. It didn't matter because she ended up trading the dog for pot and she never fell in love with me. (Yes, you read that correctly. She traded our dog, for pot. WHAT KIND OF A SICK BITCH TRADES A DOG FOR POT?!)

The point is being fat made me a nice guy. I'm a natural giver. I like helping people out and making them happy. And I really like that about myself.

I can't say that I have ever gotten over my ADD. I still can't focus. I just learned how to work through it and work harder so that I could outperform anyone else in my game. I will admit that sometimes I do it just to stick my tongue out and spit on anyone who once thought I was lazy. Whatever the motivation, I have a sick skill set. I can understand and write computer programs in any language. I can create websites in my sleep. I administrate DNS, virtual hosts, email servers, load balancers and anything in between.

But the most important part is that I did learn to like myself even when *you* might have thought I was disgusting. When I was seated in the middle seat, my fat falling over into your 12A area, I stopped hearing your comments or worrying that your panties were in a bundle. That takes the kind of strength and character which real courage is made of.

So when I put myself out there on my blog or in a speech and someone doesn't like it, I could not frickin' care less.

Being fat gave me an edge. Let's review:

1. I learned to be a giver.
2. I developed an insane work ethic.
3. I am brave and confident.

Maybe you still don't understand, but that's your loss and I no longer have any desire to punch you in the face. Screw that. Just because I'm a nice guy and all that doesn't make me a pacifist wuss. If you are going to fuck with me, you'd better do your worst because I will certainly do mine. Bet on that.

Keep reading.

4

Ahoy Motherfucking Misfits

It's more fun to be a pirate than to join the Navy.

- STEVE JOBS

I 'm just going to go ahead and say it— I have the innards of a superhero. I don't mean I have supersonic sperm or a bionic colon or anything weird like that. I'm talking about guts. I've got as much guts as any superhero ever had. A lot of that came through living life as a disabled and ridiculed fatty, but some of it just came from me, born with an appetite for speed and risk and an inability to follow the rules. And when you live like that, always looking over your shoulder for a second here and there to see if you're going to get caught, you become so brave that you're willing to try almost anything. So you might get caught. Worse things could happen, I've been told.

I don't mean that I don't like rules. I honestly mean that my brain doesn't work inside the lines of the rules. Let's say, for example, that you sat me down to explain the rules of a new game. Frickin' Parcheesi. Whatever. Doesn't matter. The minute you started to explain the game my brain would begin mapping out the angles to get around the rules and how I could get to the end faster than you. And guess what? I would win, not by luck or good skill, but because I would figure out how to bend the rules.

I don't do rules.

I don't like games.

Scratch the second one.

It's not that I don't *like* games; it's just that I won't play any game unless I can find a way to cheat. I just don't work any other way. One thing that tells me—as sure as my morning shit—is that I wouldn't last a day in the military. Thank you, honorable men and women for joining the armed forces, but I'm a pirate kind of guy. I just am. For me, "the honor's in the dolla', kid!" I don't want to be a soldier. I want to be a pirate living by quotes from *The Boiler Room*.

I guess I was in the tenth grade when I ran my first angle. Well, that's not exactly true. I ran all sorts of schemes before that, I'm just going to start in seventh grade because that's the first time I made—what I remember as—a good deal of cash. It started with selling candy. I was *that* kid—the one with the business in my backpack because there was demand. I would buy Now and Laters at the store, getting 6 pieces for ninety-nine cents and then I'd turn around and toss them to kids in the hallways for fifty cents per. That's 2 bucks profit: a fantastic margin for a 13 year old.

One day I had an idea to expand my operation to sell Fleer baseball cards. It was a perfect commodity. They were light to carry around, cheap to buy in bulk, and everyone was into them. This was 1989, which is significant if you know ANYTHING about baseball. That was a banner rookie year with guys like Ken Griffey, Jr. and Gary Sheffield and Randy Johnson just starting out. So if you bought a cheap pack of trading cards it was totally possible that you would hook a great rookie card. The Griffey card, for example, was instantly valuable. You could go and sell it outright to a collector for twenty bucks as soon as school was over. I knew that and marketed the shit out of it until I had kids buying Fleer packs like they were lottery tickets. I bought them for $2.50 per pack and resold them at $4.85. That might seem like an odd price point to you, but it just *happened* to be the same price as a

Woodrow Wilson hot lunch. That year a lot of kids skipped lunch for the thrill of quadrupling their Fleer investment.

And that could have been likely. Except it wasn't. Because what those kids didn't know was that the packs were wax sealed and really fucking easy to slip open and close up again. So every night I'd open the packs before sale, cherry pick them for the Griffeys and Sheffields and anything else that was valuable, stuff them back with crap cards and use a wet rag and iron to re-seal everything back up.

Every once in a while I made a mother pack, intentionally stuffed with aces and I would toss it to a "friend." The deal was he could keep the cards as long as he opened it someplace really public, like study hall, and made a big deal of the whole thing. He was a pretty good actor, come to think of it. He'd be like, "Holy Shit! I got a Griffey AND a Sheffield! Shoe's cards are the bomb." A genuine in-person endorsement is the best kind of ad that bribery, *I mean money*, can buy. I could have taught the whole process as a combined Business/Home Economics unit: ShoeMoney Marketing and Ironing Best Practices. It was such great idea. It made me popular and profitable all because I was willing to do what others were willing not to.

I hope you're not sick of that line yet, because you're going to hear it a lot more as we go. It's probably my strongest mantra. Be willing to do what others are willing not to do.

That was my first lesson in how to exploit people's passions for profit. My editors suggested that I use a different word so that I don't come off as such a careless prick, but I won't because exploitation is exactly what I do. I knew what the kids at school wanted—sugar and trading cards—so that's exactly that's what I provided. And it was very profitable by twelve-year-old standards. I have a knack for knowing what people want before they know they want it. That comes in really handy as a marketer and I don't think there's anything wrong with it. Call it exploitation if you want to. I do.

The following year I pulled off my great insurance graft, something so simple and fearless I am still proud of the idea today. It drives home the next big point. Yes, you have to be willing to do what others are not willing to do. That's the first thing. But you also have to be willing to do it—immediately. It's not enough just to see angles. Once you see them you have to be willing to act on them quickly and aggressively. If you are afraid, you'll probably screw it up and get caught and if you hesitate, the angle will be gone.

So now I'm fourteen and my buddy is sixteen and he's sick rich. He always had cool stuff, like a sweet ass car loaded with a $3,000 sound system (which, incidentally, I installed for him because I was just good at that type of thing—taking things apart and then putting them back together again. That's not the point here, but I'll come back to it later). In Moline a $3,000 sound system is ridiculous for anyone to have back then—let alone a sixteen year old who doesn't realize what a target that thing was. A fool's target.

That's exactly what gave me the idea.

The background on this friend was that his parents had a ton of money, but because of *this, that and the other,* well, he didn't live at home with those parents. At the time he was living with his girlfriend's parents and that's a whole 'nother story that he can tell you when he fucking writes a book. But that one detail is important for the purposes of this particular story because this girlfriend's parents are also well-off and very well respected in the community. Also, you need to know that he had a job that kept him working late at night.

OK. So knowing all of that I said to him, "Just trust me on this. We're going to take the car to my house, we'll break your window, we'll break your dash in half, we'll pull out all your electronics and the full sound system and we'll stash it in my garage."

And he looked at me like I was nuts, of course.

But I was like, "No. No. No. Seriously, trust me on this. No one will be awake when you roll in from work at midnight and they won't notice that your car is already trashed."

Still, he was looking at me with those squinty eyes no doubt thinking, "What the fuck, you crazy fat farm…"

But I didn't let him interrupt me and I kept explaining the details. "So you leave your car outside on the street like always and keep your window down so that anyone who passes by can see that it's smashed. Go inside and sit tight. At 2 am, hit the panic button on your car keys and stay fucking put in your bed."

So he did.

And when his girlfriend's parents awoke to the blaring car alarm they went out to the street to check on the noise. To their surprise, my buddy's car had been trashed and robbed. Of course they called the police immediately, reported the theft and the whole thing was chalked up to random street crime. A week later my buddy and I collected the insurance payout to buy a brand new $3,000 sound system. After buying the new system and installing it we quietly sold off the pieces of the original system. At the end, we made about a grand in profit and no one ever knew the half of it.

This worked because I saw an angle. It worked because I was willing to do what others are not willing to and because I was fearless enough to do it quickly and aggressively.

But I already knew all of those things at the time of my great insurance graft.

For me, the new lesson here was one of the most valuable lessons I ever learned—about marketing, about storytelling, about life. When someone else tells your story it is a thousand times more powerful and profound than it could ever be if you told it yourself.

I'm going to spend this entire book telling you how smart and cool and awesome I am. And that's fine. I'm a great storyteller and I'm very convincing, so I'm confident you'll believe me in the end. But if someone else posts a comment on my blog about how helpful my latest package of tips was—that's far more valuable for my brand. And if, let's say, Paris Hilton happens to tweet that, I'm the bomb, you had better believe that my website's traffic will explode and a whole crop of bomb wannabes will start paying attention to ShoeMoney. The source of information is huge. (As journalistic integrity goes to shit, we can't forget that.)

The insurance scam was an okay idea, but when I figured out how to get a third party involved, it became a fucking brilliant idea. Those parents were rich and respected. They were pillars of the damn community. Was anyone going to call them liars? Hell no. They were the law-abiding, tax paying, God-fearing, upstanding citizens with children who just happened to be the victims of street crime. That story became true because they told it that way and my angle worked specifically because I knew that's how it would go.

Be aggressive and bold. Have a little imagination and don't be stupid.

Side Note: I hate that fucking line from Forrest Gump. What the hell does, "Stupid is as stupid does," mean? It's stupid, is what it is. Don't ever quote it to me.

But I couldn't call myself a respectable misfit without sharing at least one stupid story. Trust me, I've got a few. Not counting all my crafty angling and strategic risks as well as the stress that 400 pounds of fat puts on a guy, sometimes I'm surprised that I survived the simple recklessness of my youth at all. I don't believe in luck, really. But one particular night I was both stupid and reckless and really lucky.

From the time I was fourteen to the time I was in my twenties my father lived in Ohio. After his escapades with his two companies he had an opportunity to return to a fully functional International

Harvester factory to work and become eligible for his full pension. And he took it, but left our family's roots in Moline. So my mom would go there all the time on the weekends to be with him. This left my sister and me home alone with tons of opportunities to be reckless and stupid. And oh yea, we could also hide things (like stolen stereo equipment) in the garage. Our weekends of freedom were also perfect for hosting keg parties.

On the weekend of Homecoming I hosted one such party, which got absolutely dumb nuts. Somehow the tapper on the keg got busted mid-party. So I called my friend, Nick, who worked at the Holiday Inn, to lend us a tapper and save our buzzes. He agreed to leave one by the hotel backdoor so a bunch of us hopped into my truck and headed over there to grab it.

At this point, I realized that we weren't buzzed at all. We were COMPLETELY TRASHED. And as I headed in through the backdoor of the Holiday Inn, the rest of the guys stayed in the parking lot, busy shooting out windows and tires with my M16 bb gun. We all thought it was completely hilarious. And that's when I saw the bar. In the corner of the backroom where Nick had left the tap I saw a huge, shiny, bar on wheels. It was stainless steel with three full kegs in the refrigerated bottom and three shelves of unopened booze on the top— Captain, Absolut, Jack. Everything. There was a sign taped to the cabinet that said, "Johnson Wedding." I pulled off the sign and rolled the entire bar out the back door.

Somehow our drunken group hoisted this huge bar up and into the back of my pickup and we all made it home to keep the party going strong.

Three hours later we were ever more COMPLETELY TRASHED. That's about the time when my buddy, Russ Hoffman, had a *great* idea. Now Russ is a good enough guy, but he was a complete idiot when he got drunk. This particular night he was obviously wasted and stupid, but he was also royally pissed off because he had been cut from the soccer team that afternoon.

Once the party thinned out the remaining crew—Russ, Jim Geyer and Matt Winters—convinced me to go on a "joy ride" through the town. We took Russ' car. Actually it was more like a tank. I swear you could fit fourteen guys in that thing and it was all steel with a little fake wood paneling.

In the back of our high school's grounds the soccer team had a "kick back" wall, which was the exact size of a goal but made of solid wood. This made quick kicking drills really efficient during practice because the ball would "kick back" at you without needing a goalie to chase anything down. That wall was also the place where the soccer team would hang out. It was their symbolic place.

None of these details were on my mind at the time as we were just goofing around, I thought. We were speeding around in the tank, shooting the shit out of things and throwing beer cans out the windows. Suddenly, out of nowhere, the wagon is off the road.

The next thing I know, our tank is on the athletic field, barreling towards the kick back wall at about 65 miles per hour. Russ yells like a retarded cowboy, "Shoe, we're gonna' slice through it like butter. Those soccer fucks are screwed!"

I shouted back, "What the fuck, dude?! What the fuck?! WHAT THE FUCK?!?"

I was looking to the other guys to help out a little bit, but they were just rooting Russ on and making the situation worse. Finally, I heard another voice in the car scream, "Don't worry man. We did this before." And boom. Just like that we crashed into the soccer wall.

The front of that tank crumpled up like a piece of paper.

All I really remember from the first few seconds was thinking, "Oh my god. Oh my god. Oh my god...Am I alive? Am I actually alive? Oh my god. Is anything broken? Oh my god."

Yes. We were alive. I'm not sure how, but we had all survived, mostly unbroken. So much of it had to be just dumb luck. Geyer had been riding shotgun and I was right behind him in the backseat. None of us were wearing seatbelts. When we hit the wall my massive body went flying into the Geyer's chair and actually broke the seat's weld. If I hadn't been so fat, I still would have flown into the chair, but probably would have pinned Geyer's body between the steel frame of the chair and the exposed steel of the front dash. I'm sure he survived only because my body broke the chair between us. Winters was sitting to my left and ended up with a broken leg. Retard Russ left the deal without a scrape. I was badly bruised all over my body, but nothing was broken.

So maybe now you can understand how my body busted the steel frame of car seat.

We were a little banged up, but mostly, we were shocked.

What Russ and Geyer and Winters didn't know was that after the last time they rammed the kick back wall the soccer parents rebuilt it. When they rebuilt it, they added a 2 foot concrete slab in between the wood panels for reinforcement against idiotic drunk assholes who might think ramming a car into the practice equipment was a good idea.

It is still unbelievable when I think about it. It's crazy that we survived. It was even crazier that, with a completely collapsed hood, the wagon's engine still turned over when Russ cranked the key. We were able to drive just far enough to stash the crumpled-up mess of a car in a friend's nearby garage, limp back to my house and keep the party going. Once we got back to my house, we were greeted with high fives and shots of Jack reconfirming our thoughts that we were invincibly awesome.

When Monday morning rolled around I went to school without a care in the world—not concerned with the stolen bar in my garage or the broken kick back wall at school. We probably would have gotten away with Russ' soccer revenge if we hadn't left the wagon's license plate at the scene of the crime. As it turned out, the license plate had fallen off with the impact and we were too busy feeling lucky and awesome to have noticed.

So they had nailed Russ and as soon as they threatened jail he sang like a canary about Tim and Matt and me. We all got hauled out of first period and were taken down to the station in cuffs. To be honest, when it was all first going down we felt like the whole ordeal was a big joke. We didn't take it seriously—at all. The next thing we know they are taking our mug shots and we're hooting like monkeys and screaming out our aliases for the cops to note. We were the Dangerous Crew made up of Terminator X (Russ' homage to Public Enemy),

MacGyver (obviously for Geyer), Summers (cuz' he was Winters) and me—Shamu.

So frickin' funny.

And then they booked us with felony criminal trespassing and the penalty of jail time. I guess that's when it finally stopped being funny.

I ended up spending one night in jail but because I didn't have any prior criminal marks, my sentence was reduced to court supervision, a long school suspension and a promise to rebuild the soccer dicks' wall. I did everything as I was directed, including personally apologizing to each member of the soccer team and their parents. My mom drove me from house to house. That was a fun afternoon.

I promised myself I would be smarter, that I wouldn't get myself into that position again. And if I did pull something illegal, at least I wouldn't get caught next time. It is possible to be reckless and rebellious **and smart**, you know.

Oh, but I forgot about Nick at the Holiday Inn.

He ended up getting into major hot water for the missing bar and finally ratted me out. I wasn't mad at him, though. It actually didn't matter that he gave me up since the hotel had the whole thing on their video surveillance anyhow. The manager turned out to be a really cool guy too. He called me up and basically slapped me on the hand. He told me just to return it, which I did, and he never spoke another word about the whole thing to another soul.

That was a crazy night. I realized I got lucky. I realized that I wanted to be smarter and that it was probably time to grow up a little bit after all of that. And I did. But I never grew out of being a misfit and a rule bender. It's just who I am and how I work.

I'm not calling myself Steve Jobs here—and even if I did, we have already learned that wouldn't be effective unless Mark Zuckerberg called me such. So, as I said, I'm definitely not calling myself Steve Jobs, but in a lot of ways I know he operated a lot like me, and he was never squeaky clean either. It was a part of his mantra to be a misfit. He said it time and time again.

> Here's to the crazy ones, the misfits, the rebels, the troublemakers, the round pegs in the square holes…the ones who see things differently—they're not fond of rules. You can quote them, disagree with them, glorify or vilify them, but the only thing you can't do is ignore them because they change things…because the ones who are crazy enough to think that they can change the world, are the ones who do.
>
> - Steve Jobs

I'm not saying that I'm a world changer. I'm just saying that I'm definitely crazy enough and gutsy enough and so far, I've been lucky enough to maybe do just that in the end.

Ahoy.

5

Lessons from Being (Almost) Killed

I spit phrases that'll thrill you,

You're nobody till somebody kills you.

     -NOTORIOUS B.I.G. (Again)

I'm not dead.

Clearly.

No one actually killed me, as it turned out. They just *almost* did. And it was crazy. I mean CRA-ZY. You have no idea until someone almost kills you.

And I'm not talking about nearly *dying*. That's a totally different thing. I have probably been close to that a lot too, bringing it on myself. I drank a ton. I did a lot of drinking and driving (which in rural-*ish* America is considered normal behavior and not a dangerous crime). I also dabbled in drugs, pills, whatever. And then of course, I was really frickin' fat, which isn't good for anyone's overall health. Let's just say that I had a general carelessness for my self-preservation. I was a lot like Johnny Knoxville, just less videotaped.

But I'm not talking about almost dying. This story is about the time that someone came at me—guns firing, Compton style—and almost *killed* me. (That's why I was insistent about including another Biggie

Smalls quote, even though I was told that it's bad form to double dip like that. No one else could say it better. Damn he was a talented lyricist.)

I don't like fluff. So I promise that everything I'm writing here has a purpose and value. Not like my friend, Tim Ferriss. I can totally call him out, because I told him the same exact thing to his face when I had him on my radio show to plug his book, *The 4-Hour Workweek*. He's a great guy and his book is really smart. But it's about a hundred pages longer than it needs to be (or two hours too long on audio books, as I "read"). I won't do that here. I do have a tendency to think and talk in tangents. No doubt, you've noticed that by now. That's just how my brain works, which means that's also how I write.

There might be times when you're reading and thinking, "WTF?!? Why am I suddenly reading about a mouse that lives in Jeremy's basement?" or "SERIOUSLY?!? Are you going to put in another random and long comment in parentheses?" Yes, that might seem weird, but I absolutely promise you that even if you can't understand it right at the time you're reading, there is a reason for that story and every other detail that I'm putting into this book. (Actually, for that very reason, I decided to take out the story about the mouse, which came a few chapters later, even though it's frickin' hilarious, but I'm leaving in the nod to Notorious.) Context is important for you to really get where I'm coming from and who I am. The way that someone chooses to tell a story matters as well. So what you're getting here in this book isn't just my stories. You're getting a little Jeremy time. And with that comes tangents. You can expect that there will be a lot of tangents in your future and they will all be worth your time.

Okay, so I'm getting to the story about the dudes with the guns. That's the really exciting part, but first I have to tell you one other thing.

I already told you that as a kid I probably should have been diagnosed with ADD, or however it's termed these days. I definitely still have that, whatever it's called. It's nearly impossible for me to focus, like a normal person, on the everyday type stuff like listening to anyone who's talking to me. My brain buzzes around and can't sit still with one thing. That's the first part of my issue. The other half of the problem is the exact opposite. Call it tunnel vision, if you want. So I have extreme ADD with a side of tunnel vision. What a fun cranial value pack, let me tell you. My brain is going, going, going, going, speeding along until—**BAM**—it slams against something really interesting to me and I stop (with a lot of whiplash) and see nothing else, but that **ONE THING**. Once I tunnel into something, nothing else exists and nothing else can tear me away.

I'm not happy with that explanation. I am not convinced that you really understand my brain…yet.

Remember when George Bush (Senior) used the metaphor, *A thousand points of light,* in some speech? I don't remember what the hell he was talking about, but the image is a good one. If you could see inside my head (How badass would that be?!) and actually watch the ideas sparking like actual points of light (I should ask my wife, the doctor, how long until we can actually do this?), at any given moment my brain would look like an apocalyptic meteor shower. Let me try this once more. We haven't been through an apocalyptic meteor shower, so that's probably not going to help us much here.

Remember the static energy ball from the science museum field trip? The one with the blue electric rays that shoot from the center of the ball and make your hair stand out like you were Dee Snider in the 80s. Now imagine that ball and the blue rays. (It's technically called a Van de Graaff generator so don't say you didn't fucking learning a thing from reading this book, okay? I'm hitting you over the head with value, even in my tangents.) If you have a normal brain, it probably spits out ideas at a speed of 1. Blue rays zap out every once in a while. So if you're at a 1, I'm at a speed of 150. Imagine the blue rays—frickin' thoughts firing away like pandemonium. Spew. Spew. Spew. Spew. Spew. All disconnected. Random. It makes you dizzy.

That's

                                              Attention.

Deficit.

                                              Disorder.

Until…

I find something.

ONE THING.

To focus

ON.

When I get that one thing that attracts my focus, all the energy that was going in 150 different directions before, comes together like a laser. Then I'm like Obi-Wan wielding a lightsaber.

Completely.

Totally.

Focused.

And BADASS!

That's what I'm talking about. That's what I'm capable of and what you need to understand about my way of thinking.

There are lots of practical applications for the kind of focus I can wield.

For example, you can become a video game wizard. I did this with NHL Hockey. All I did for months in junior high was sit in front of the game and play. I mean I ate and shit and slept sometimes, but I don't remember doing any of that. I just remember playing NHL

Hockey. The controller became like—what do you call it? You know, it was like another part of my body–like my elbow or my dick. You don't have to think about how to use your elbow or your dick. You just use them as you need them and they do their thing. I played so much NHL hockey that I didn't have to think about how my fingers were moving on the controller. It just all moved together. I played that game until I declared myself the best NHL Hockey player in the world. I played my friends without a goalie and won. Once I played blind-folded. What can I say? I was a prodigy, like Mozart—not because I was born to be a gamer, but because when one thing gets my attention it's like I was telling you. It's all I see and care about. When you are that focused on anything you can become great at it, I think.

When I am that focused, I become the best.

Besides NHL Hockey, I was also completely fascinated by electronics. The mechanics of how something works is just about the coolest thing to me. I have always loved taking shit apart, seeing how it was wired, experimenting with other ways to doctor the connections, making something new. I really liked messing around with the AC power in our house—AC as in alternating current, not air conditioning. But that can lead to things like electrical fires and is probably not a great idea. You can pretty easily burn down your parents' house or kill yourself when you mess around with the AC power. My mom realized that pretty quickly and bought me an AC/DC transformer, which I could use to mess around with car electronics and 12 volt stuff. That distraction helped me keep my promise to leave the house alone.

So when I was about thirteen (and couldn't technically drive yet), I bought a bunch of car *stuff*. I got a car stereo, an amp and speakers. Then I built my own custom deck—which I installed, obviously, in my waterbed. I also wired low glows for under the bed, just to complete the effect that I had—what I would call—the most supped up non-car waterbed in the Quad City area. Whatever. It was fucking awesome and I know you're jealous. And oh no, I didn't stop there. Then I devised a security system so that if someone came downstairs it would trip a wire and I would know. I also wired up the house phone so that whenever anyone called, it would beep my pager and I could listen in to whoever was talking, but they couldn't hear me.

Everyone is born being good at something. I was never good at school, but I was naturally good at electronics. As I was telling you before, somehow I managed to graduate high school—pretty much by the skin of my teeth and a lot of mercy from the people who loved my mom. Her dream was that I'd go to college, like everyone else. I couldn't imagine anything worse. I might have been content sitting on my ass for a few years, playing more Nintendo but that's not how it works after high school. Not in my house, anyway. I had to apply myself.

I had to get creative to put together some kind of plan that didn't involve college.

I found a place in Daytona called The Installer's Institute. This place was the only one of its kind. They taught you how to do everything related to car audio systems from design, to construction, to installation. You have to remember that this was in a basically pre-computer era. The concept of the computer existed and super computers were being used in little corners of the industry, but they weren't a part of everyday life and they definitely weren't—at this point—in your car. This meant that each system of the car operated independently and had to be calculated and designed and then installed, manually.

There is an art to matching the audio system with the acoustics and the resonating frequency within the body of a specific car. It's all math. It was a perfect combination for my skill set at 18. (Oh wait, I forget to tell you that the one thing I did like in school was math.) Anyhow, this program lasted two months and I was in heaven the whole time. Forget that it was the first time I was really away from home on my own—I felt for the first time in my life that I was in my element—and this element was real and valuable and applicable. The courses were in wiring and soldering. I learned how to calculate speakers to match with enclosures that would maximize sound quality. I learned how to mold abs plastic for custom dashes and door mounts and all about sound pressure levels. I was completely captivated and focused. I was great, immediately. After the first week I got so good that I blew everyone away.

In the third week we were supposed to be wiring practicals that came in from junk yards but instead my instructor put me to work on a Lamborghini Diablo that was brought in by some big-time financial dude for a customized audio overhaul. I had been there three weeks and they had me working on the Lamborghini because I could do a better job than any of my instructors. I know—I'm a Mozart prodigy. I told you. My teachers loved me. Let me say that again. It just feels so good to a guy that was pretty much despised by every other teacher in his life. My teachers frickin' loved me—what a revelation.

I completed the program and went back to Moline with a golden ticket in my hand. I could basically cherry pick the job I wanted because no one in a three state radius had been to this Institution. Not only did I have a natural electronic "geekiness," after graduating from the Installer's Institution I also had legitimate "working papers" that say I'm as good as I say I am.

Which brings me to the point at which you can fully appreciate the story of how I was almost killed.

Again, I assume that you don't know much about Moline and its surrounding areas unless you're from that area (or the surrounding areas) and if you are—well then, I am sorry. Let's just say it's not exactly a country club land. Moline itself if very blue collar and then you have Rock Island and Davenport, which nicely put, are *"not good"* areas. Not nicely put, they're shit holes. And as with most shit holes, there are lots of drugs. And where there are lots of drugs, there are gangs. But when you're used to that you kind of shit, you stop seeing it as a thing—or as anything at all.

After my two months of training in Dayton I was back in the shit-hole and its surrounding shit-hole areas. I accepted a job at a place called Sound Advice. I admit that the name was kind of gay, but the shop was the best and worked on all the sickest cars. We had tons of business because lots of black dudes lived in the area. If you don't know this already, I can explain. Black dudes love sick sound systems, especially in their cars. I am not stereotyping here, because when you observe something to be real over and over and over again—then it's not a stereotype; it's an honest, non-racist observation. Well maybe it is a little racist. I don't even know if I know what is and is not racist anymore. Beside the point, I certainly don't mean this in a negative way. In my opinion, people who like sick sound systems in their car are cool. I have a crazy sick system in my car. I always have. And I am cool, ergo, whatever. I'm making an observation in my story. Nothing more.

(Quick tangent. I have to include this, because, well, because I want to and I'm putting the whole thing in parentheses since it has nothing to do with the progression of this one story. You could completely skip this if you want. That being said, my editors don't like that last paragraph for many reasons. They argued with me to cut it completely. They say that it is an affront to people from the Quad Cities and to black people and oh yeah, also to gay people because I said that Sound Advice was kind of a "gay" name. Well I come from Moline, so I can talk about it however I want. I already explained the second. I'm not being racist when I'm talking about an observable trend. Lastly, I like to use the word "gay." I use it to mean lame, stupid, dumb, pointless, idiotic, and/or annoying. I'm using it as slang like I use the word, "sick." It's not literal, okay? I'm not using it to make any judgment on being gay or a gay lifestyle or any of my gay friends. I just like using that word that way and this is my book, so much to the dismay of my editors and my PR people I'm going to use the word, "gay," from time to time in my book. If you are offended, well, just keep reading and maybe you'll understand and forgive me. If not, you'll certainly have enough dirt on my past, my life and my general view on it that you can throw mud all over me and my blog. That's your prerogative. I've been through worse. Like being almost killed. So I'm going back to my story now with the full right to use any language that I choose and to tell things how they happened without pausing to apologize for unintentionally slurring people who are gay or black or who live in Moline.)

I had a blast working at Sound Advice because I worked on some of the sickest cars I have ever seen. One time this dude brought in a Jeep Cherokee, which okay, I admit, doesn't sound that cool to start with. But he wasn't just any dude and it wasn't just any jeep. This dude was a major dealer from Davenport and his car was a fucking solid gold Cherokee. I'm not shitting you. It was entirely gold plated with gold rims and freaking gold in the snowflake of the paint. He brought it into the shop really late at night, handed me the keys and ten grand in cash. Now never mind the fact that I had never seen ten grand in cash before (have you?), the wild part is that he says to me, "I need a car to drive." I handed him the keys to my blazer.

Long story short—he took my rusted out blazer and I drove home from work in the gold Jeep. And when I got home, I put his gold ride in my mom's garage because I'm not a gang banging thug and my ass would be shot so fast if I was caught driving that thing around. I mean, I'd be dead if I scratched it or even breathed on it wrong. I told you, I'm not fronting anything here. I'm just telling the story. But I want you to understand that this kind of stuff became totally common place. I never thought about where the money was coming from and who I was dealing with or anything. I was just having fun at my job.

I had been working late at the shop on another random night just finishing up the last connections on a job when I heard a guy cussing like crazy outside the garage. When I looked outside I saw these two huge black dudes standing outside of a '78 Olds that was completely pimped out, Huggy Bear style with 22" Daytons. I'm fascinated by the car so I keep watching and the one guy is still screaming, "Mother Fucker. Fucker. Fucker. Fucker."

He walked up to the garage and smashed his fist into the wall just to the left of the window where I was snooping. Obviously, I take this as a good time to stick my nose in their business and so I walked outside to meet them. When you picture this scene in your imagination, I want you to remember that I'm an obese dude—a hulk in my own right—but standing next to these big thug dudes I felt like a wussy runt.

Here's how the next ten minutes went down:

Me: "Are you guys okay?"

Thug Dude: *Bringing one hand up to his mouth, he paused for a second, looked me up and down and starts to rub his chin and says,* "I locked the keys in the car."

Me: "Uh, do you want me to call someone to, you know, to help?"

Thug Dude: *Staring at the ground and then at the trunk and then at the ground and then straight in my eyes.* "There's stuff in the trunk. If someone sees…it will be…………………bad."

Me: "Where are the keys at—exactly?"

Thug Dude: "In the ignition."

> *Dramatic*………………………………………………………
> ……………………………………………………*Pause.*

Me: "I'm um…I'm really good at breaking into cars. Do you want me to…?"

Thug Dude: *Interrupting me;* "Yes."

Another dramatic…………………………………………………………*pause while I consider the possible bad ways this can go down.*

Me: "Ummmm....I just want you to know that I might...well....I mean...I might..."

Thug Dude: *Interrupting me again,* "Fucker, I'm breaking the window anyhow."

Me: "Okay. Good to know 'cuz that might happen."

I ran into the shop to get my slim jims (not the delicious beef jerky treat) and I'm totally revved up because breaking into cars had sort of become a little hobby of mine. I'd do it to impress my friends—as a part of my crazy fat kid persona—all the time. We'd be out at night and we'd pass a Jiffy Lube and I'd go, "Dude, I can totally break into that car." And I'd jump out and amaze a whole truck load of my friends. You never can tell, exactly, how a little skill might come in handy down the road.

So I walk up to the car, work my magic for a minute and easily pop the lock. I felt it go "click" and the door swung open into the very happy hands of the thug. I thought for a second he was going to hug me because his arms flew up in relief. But he didn't and I was relieved, myself, because as his arms flew up I saw the piece, which was tucked into his belt. I never knew what was in the trunk. I didn't care. I was ready for them to leave right about then.

The thug dude thanked me over and over and all I could say was, "Hey, no worries," as I was trying to back away from the whole deal. He reached into the breast pocket of his leather jacket and pulled out some bills. He handed me two, yes TWO HUNDRED DOLLAR BILLS. And again I said, "Hey....no....no worries." They climbed back into the '78 Olds with the 22" Daytons and drove off.

I finally let myself exhale and smile. Two hundred dollars was more than two weeks' pay at the time.

And that was that.

I never expected to see them again.

A few weeks later I was in the garage working on a job. The garage was directly behind the showroom. I was crammed under a black Jeep Cherokee wiring a remote start when I heard what I thought was firecrackers. **POP. POP. Pop-pop-pop-pop-pop.** Just like that, at first. And then it stopped. Tim, the guy who owned the shop, was a jack ass and he was always pulling some random stupid shit. I didn't really think much of it. *Must be random stupid shit.* I just kept working.

And then it started again. Except this time it didn't sound like firecrackers any more. It was too fast and loud and continuous.

POP.POP.POP.POP.POP.POP.POP.POP.POP
POP.POP.POP.POP.POP.POP.POP.POP.POP
POP.POP.POP.POP.POP.POP.POP.POP.POP
POP.POP.POP.POP.POP.POP.POP.POP.POP
POP.POP.POP.POP.POP.POP.POP.POP.POP
POP.POP.POP.POP.POP.POP.POP.POP.POP
POP.POP.POP.POP.POP.POP.POP.POP.POP

It sounded like an Uzi submachine gun going off. Well, turns out that it *sounded like* an Uzi submachine gun going off because it *was* an Uzi submachine gun going off in the show room twenty feet from where I was, wedged underneath the carriage of that car, tucking wires into place.

Side Note: I was told that I put too many **POP**s up there and that you'd get the point with two – three lines, but then I said to that person, "Have you ever heard an Uzi going off?" And of course he hadn't so then I was like, "I should have put a whole page of **POP**s because the shots came off so frickin' fast in a matter of a few seconds. And since we're on the subject, there really should be a different word than "**POP**" to use to describe the sound because it doesn't do it justice even when I put it all in caps and bold it and write it fifty times.

So, to the person who said there were too many **POP**s, you don't know what you're talking about until you hear an Uzi going off twenty feet away from you. And when and if you do, please listen to it very closely and tell me which word would be better, okay?

There was a wall between the showroom and the garage but the curious thing about bullets that are fired from machine guns is that they break shit like glass and plastic and metal and human flesh. That day the bullets tore up everything in the showroom: all the speakers, soundboards, car decks, display cases and windows. And then the bullets began to break through the wall between the showroom and the garage until the walls started to crumble and there were gaping holes.

This is the point when my trust in life—you know, that trust and confidence we all walk around with every day that we don't even really notice but which makes us absolutely certain that this one ordinary day is surely not the last day of our life—completely crumbled.

Okay, so now that I've made a big point about the sound of the bullets being fired I have to correct myself. When I think about it, about what I actually heard when my brain registered what was happening around me, I don't actually remember hearing the specific shots. I just remember hearing the clink of the casings as they fell on the floor like metal hail. It's kind of like in every war movie which has a scene with a vicious ambush and it's always shown like it's happening in slow motion. Every sense you have has gone numb except for one.

When I realized what was happening—that I was in the middle of a retaliation shoot out because the owner of Sound Advice was really fucking deep into the drug world and he somehow fucked someone over which meant that, unfortunately, I was going to get shot by an Uzi and die any second—all I heard was that clinking.

Clink.

Clink.

Clink.

That noise completely attached me to one focusing thought: *I'm dead.*

I'm dead. I'm dead. I'm dead. I'm dead.

And then it stopped. For just a second, everything was silent and my thought was still the same (but with a half of a question mark at the end) *I'm...dead?*

Which, of course, I wasn't because I remember that I was still holding these two wires in between my fingers and dead jerks can't hold wires. But it takes a minute to register big things like whether or not you're dead. I guess I registered that I was not dead when I heard someone yell, "Get the fuck out here you little bitch!"

More gunshots.

Were they screaming at me? I had no idea. I couldn't move. I was frozen under the car holding those wires like they were my salvation.

"You think you can fucking fuck us, asshole?"

I'm still under the car.

"You are fucked fucker."

Holding the wires. *I'm fucked. I'm fucking fucked. I'm dead. I'm dead. I'm dead. I'm dead. I'm dead. Hold the wires. Hold the wires. Hold the wires.*

"We'll be back mother fucker...to fuck you."

I'm dead. I'm dead. I'm dead. I'm dead.

"Nigga, let's go! LET'S GO!"

I'm dead. I'm dead. I'm dead. I'm dead.

And then they kicked the door open and ran into the garage. I was still under the car. I knew the first thing they saw were my fat feet sticking out from under the Jeep. But I couldn't move a thing. I was frozen, holding those two wires between my fingers.

I'm dead. I'm dead. I'm dead. I'm dead.

Holy shit. I'm dead.

They ran past me towards the back door and I heard sirens. The sirens were close.

Holy shit. This is really it. I'm dead. I'm dead. I'm dead. I'm still holding these wires. I'm frozen. I'm dead. I'm dead. I'm dead.

Wait…they ran past me.

They ran past me?

I'm dead?

Wait…am I dead yet?

I stuck my head out from under the car and saw the back of a big black dude, running for the exit with an Uzi in his right hand.

He got to the back door of the garage, stopped, and turned around. Our eyes locked. It was my dude—the big thug dude who locked the keys in his Olds with the 22" Daytons.

He nodded once at me, like he was saying, "Whad' up?" and then made a *"shhhhh"* symbol with his finger at his lips. Then he smiled and sliced that same finger across his throat. It wasn't hard to understand what that meant.

Hey....no worries. I can do that.

It took me about a full minute to form another thought—the most profound of my life to that point.

I'm not dead.

And that's how it happened. That's the story of how I was almost killed. In the end there isn't a whole lot more to say about it except that it's good to *not* be dead.

I fantasized a lot about being a gun blazing cowboy or a death agent ninja but the truth of it is that the real moment of life and death is scary stuff. It's cool and all when it happens in The Wire. It's a lot less cool and a lot more piss-your-pants scary when it happens in real life. I don't care how tough you think you are; it is scary.

So, here's what we can learn from being (almost) killed:

- First, do what you are good at—no matter what it is, just do it and get really good at it.
- Second, use your talents to help other people when you can. You never know when and if your talent for breaking into cars could save your life.

- Third, *The Wire* is an awesome series. If you haven't seen it, you need to watch immediately. Seriously. Stop reading this book right now and go and find *The Wire: Season One*. But don't wish to be in a shoot-out from *The Wire*. It's really freaky in real life. I don't care how tough you think you are.
- Lastly, if you do walk out of an almost being killed situation, well then, you're walking out with an incredibly awesome story that you definitely need to include when you're writing a book.

And that's that.

6
Footloose Ohio

Sure, I've been called a xenophobe, but the truth is I'm not. I honestly just feel that America is the best country and all the other countries aren't as good. That used to be called "patriotism."

-KENNY POWERS,

Kenny Powers' Motivational Tape

I realize that my chapter about the time I almost got killed has ended and this is the point where I should be moving on, but the thing about almost getting killed is that it stays with you. So there's a good chance that stuff is going to spill over into this next chapter and maybe come up sometime later in the book, too. You could say it was one of those pivotal points in life that had a major effect on what came after.

So we're not done talking about it, yet.

In case I didn't make this clear—it was a very good thing that I didn't get full-out killed. Once I realized that the thugs were gone, I was thankful and relieved. I checked my body for bullet holes and made sure my balls were still where they should be. Everything was good and I sort of congratulated myself for not only being alive but for not absolutely pissing my pants. And then I took a big deep breath.

The relief lasted about ten seconds.

Then I got paranoid.

I heard sirens. I knew that the cops were outside. I was convinced that the thug dudes were going to double back, busting back through the garage. I was sure I was still going to get hit. Either the dudes would realize that leaving a living witness was a really bad business decision and execute me on purpose *or* I would get caught in the cross fire of a dudes/cops shoot out. They might even take me as a hostage. I didn't know. I didn't exactly have time to reason through a bunch of scenarios. I just felt that I was going to be a goner. Any second.

I pulled myself out from under the Cherokee and scanned the garage for some type of weapon to defend myself. I only found one. I grabbed a pneumatic nail gun off the tool chest, planted my feet and took aim at the back door.

That's exactly how the cops found me when they busted in.

Now, hold on. You have to know what a pneumatic nail gun is to appreciate this part of the story. It's the tool we used to nail speaker boxes shut. The nails came out fast and had pretty good range but they're like—maybe—an inch long. We used to have nail gun wars in the garage when business was slow, and you're getting to know how I am so you can probably expect that I had gotten pretty fucking expert with my aim, which I had. Even so, even with perfect aim and pretty good range, this was still like going to war with a staple gun. I figured that I'd be able to pop one of the thugs right in the eye and do some type of damage, at least. Maybe it would distract them enough to get away. I had to try to defend my life somehow, even if it meant going ballistic with a gay little nail gun.

And so, as I was saying, that's exactly how the cops found me when they busted in.

I thought it was pretty funny, especially when I think about it now—me all hard-ass with my gay little nail gun. But the dozen or so cops that charged in weren't laughing. They came in from both doors and surrounded me with their assault rifles, all tough and bullshit. Now Moline, as I have explained, isn't exactly the land of a thousand country clubs. There's plenty of shit that happens there to keep the cops working (like kids' ramming cars into soccer "kick backs" and boosting stocked bars from the local Holiday Inn and other random midnight vandalism). But a car shop getting shot to hell over the matter of a lot of missing cocaine is a major situation. Moline, Chicago, New York, South Central. Wherever. It would be a major situation anywhere so these cops were completely jerking off that they were in the middle of it.

They had me surrounded, twelve cops staring me down with their assault rifles. They then went through the whole spiel exactly like I had heard it a thousand times on Cops. Honestly, it was MAJORLY over the top. I mean, clearly, I wasn't the bad guy in this situation. I WAS PACKING A NAIL GUN FOR CHRIST SAKE. I wasn't the one that shot up the whole damn place. That had to have been obvious, even to a bunch of retards.

But I was the only one for them to surround so I dropped my "weapon," and they threw me to the ground. They spread my legs and put my hands over my head. Then someone came down with his full weight on my back and I took a really sharp knee in my back. You never realize how sharp a knee can be until it pounds directly into the center of your spine. Apparently, some cowboy cop was really jizzed up and making a show of the whole thing. It totally knocked my wind out. They screamed the same questions at me over and over again. "Where's the cocaine? Who else is here? Where's the cocaine? Who else is here?" But I couldn't catch my breath to even give them a frickin' answer.

Finally I managed a pissy, "I don't know."

But they kept screaming.

That idiot's knee was still in my back and I was getting more pissed by the second so I screamed back—a lot more pissed off this time, "I DON'T KNOW!"

Eventually this whole back and forth got old and one of the cops said he recognized me from around town. That calmed the whole crew down enough to break the screaming stand-off. They cuffed me and took me to the station where I was drilled with more questions. They tried to "Law & Order" me for a few hours until they realized that I really didn't know anything about what had just gone down at Sound Advice. Honestly, I didn't know anything about the drugs or the racket that Tim, my boss, had been running.

It turned out that, besides being a jackass, Tim was also a major cocaine distributer. Sound Advice was basically a front for the Midwest's main distribution point. Let me put it another way. Pretty much any cocaine that made its way to Chicago at that time first came through Tim. And I had no frickin' clue. Even though tons of jacked up black dudes with fancy cars were in and out of the shop, always flashing lots of cash, I was oblivious. I mean, automatically assuming they were all drug dealers would be racist, right? We've been over that. So besides the obvious stuff that I had basically ignored, the only piece of information that I really had was that the thug dude had been to the shop two weeks before the night of the shooting.

That was the only thing I knew and I decided to keep it to myself. I mean, everyone knows what a slicing finger across the throat usually means. I had taken the hint and I wasn't voluntarily offering myself up into all that crap. But the cops kept throwing more information at me, trying to intimidate me into telling them something else. From all that information I was able to piece together the full Sound Advice story.

Tim was a major cocaine distributor, but not a very smart businessman. He screwed somebody over, somehow, and owed money to a big guy in Chicago. The thug dudes worked for that big guy and the time they drove down in their Olds with the 22" Daytons they had come to threaten Tim or to squeeze him for a payment or something to that effect. Apparently that didn't work, because they came back looking for Tim and a bunch of cocaine. When they didn't find what they wanted, I guess they got frustrated. The place was empty so they shot it all to hell.

But they left me alive.

I was alive and that's what the cops couldn't understand. I think that's why they thought I was involved. That was the only logical explanation for leaving a living witness. That was the sticking point that night and that's what they wanted me to explain.

Did I know those guys? Had I seen their faces? Could I ID them?

The right answers—of course—were: Yes. Yes. Yes. But I was like, "Naw man. I don't know."

I didn't want to be involved. I told them that I didn't know anything about the drugs. (True). I told them I never met anyone (Lie). I told them I didn't see any faces. I said I was working under a car and they were wearing hoodies over their faces. (Lie. True. Lie.)

Tim had turned State's Evidence and was going to testify against this big guy from Chicago. They needed another witness to strengthen the case. They wanted me to be that guy. They wanted me to identify the thug dudes. They told me that if I didn't help them put all these guys away, that I was a dead man. They told me stories about the kind of business these guys were involved with. They told me how serious they were. They told me that they were definitely already looking for me. They told me I didn't have a chance without the protection of the state. They told me I had to be a part of the case.

That's the thing about being *almost* killed. Even though you're alive, you're still really pretty screwed. I knew that the cops were right about my chances. I knew that I wouldn't be a hard dude to find. I knew they would have to come looking for me and when they found me they'd put a bullet in my head and then maybe stuff me in the trunk of a car with 22" Daytons.

But I didn't want any part of that case. There was no way I was going into witness protection. I've seen enough movies to know that never works, anyhow. I couldn't stay put either, though. I knew that for sure. I didn't want a bullet in my head. So I picked a third option.

Ohio.

My dad was living in Ohio at the time. I decided to move my ass out there with him and disappear into the middle of nowhere. In retrospect, a bullet in the head would have definitely been less painful than a year in Catawba, Ohio.

Let me help you get a better understanding of what living in the middle of nowhere is like. The closest gas station is 40 miles away, which means that when you have a half of a tank of gas you better plan on hiking back to the gas station pretty soon because it will take you nearly that much fuel to get there. The "village" officially measures 0.3 square miles wide, which is equal to 192 acres. Hell if I know what an acre is. I think it's maybe a little smaller than a football field.

I Googled some other stuff to help you get a grasp on the size and this is what I got: Central Park sits on 843 acres in the middle of the island of Manhattan. Andy Griffin based Small Town USA of Mayberry on his childhood home in a place called Mount Airy, North Carolina. That place is 5376 acres. Frickin' Disney World takes up 25,000 acres! And let me promise you that Catawba, on its 192 acres, is no magical wonderland.

Let me think. What could be worse than living in the middle of nowhere? Oh! I know! Living in the middle of nowhere with your dad IN A HOUSE TRAILER! It wasn't like he was poor. He made a lot of money but instead of investing in a house he put money into guns, ammunition, beer, dump trucks and a back hoe for pond digging. My room was smaller than a jail cell and the bathroom felt like a port-o-potty.

So, let me say that Ohio wasn't exactly like Heaven with all the virgins and stuff that are there. (Oh wait, I haven't gotten to that part yet and so you're probably confused. Whatever. I'm leaving the reference in anyway because this is what you call a "teaser." I know I already got your $14.95 or whatever random price point the ad junkies come up with, but I really want to you get the full value of the book—whatever you paid—so keep reading, okay? In a few chapters you'll learn about all the virgins who are waiting to have sex with you in Heaven. That has to be worth the $*Whatever*.95 you shelled out.)

So, where was I? Oh right. Living in Ohio wasn't exactly awesome. My dad didn't care what I (or anyone else) thought though. He loved to fish, hunt and be on his own. He could horde a ton of shit into this tiny little trailer and the pole barn out back. It was hell for me but it sure seemed like it was heaven for him. He got to live there the way he liked to live—doing whatever he wanted. Technically he was there because that's where one of the last International Harvester factories was operating. He had let his own two companies waste away, but he could still get his pension with a few more years of factory work. So that's what he was doing, technically.

And then I moved in.

Even though it was crowded and uncomfortable for me, I know my dad was happy to have my company When I first arrived he bought me a carton of smokes and things were as cool as they can be when you're living with your father in a house trailer in the middle of nowhere. At first I got to do whatever the hell I wanted. And for the first month, doing whatever I wanted actually meant that I was doing nothing. I'd lie in bed for hours. I'd smoke a ton and watch TV. Sometimes I jerked off. Jeez, what do you expect? There wasn't much else to do when you are living in a trailer in Catawba, Ohio. I feel like I have really made that clear.

The thing about this speck-on-the-map farming town is that it was basically like the town on Footloose. Everyone lived off these dusty dirt roads. Everyone was extremely religious and really pure and all the kids were these freaky focused athletes. They had to be. The town was so damn small every kid in the high school had to play every sport or they wouldn't have the numbers to make a full team for anything. And because the town was so small there was literally one intersection that everything was built around. That's where everyone would hang out, drinking something nutritious like, I don't know—milk, maybe.

That was the scene as I found it.

Now, I was a nineteen year old with no interest in the community or their religion or their sports teams. The only thing I was really into was my car and my car stereo. I had this beat up red 2-wheel drive Blazer and since I had nothing better to do I decided that I was going to completely pimp the thing out. I bought black pin striping to detail the sides. I took the wheels off and painted them all black. I cut out all of the rusted portions and bondoed it back together. Then I re-painted it all. And for what it was, I gotta' say, it was AWESOME. It was really fucking awesome. I'm still proud of what I did to that tin shell.

And then there was the sound system. I took out the backseats and replaced it with a huge speaker box that went all along the back and then angled to the edge of the front seats. So if you looked back all you'd see was this black slant with six subwoofers behind it. When the system was on, you could literally put a quarter on the top of my car and it would bounce up and down in the air six feet above the roof. It was so crazy. I loved it and I actually won three Pound the Pavement awards with that vehicle because the SPL level was so crazy high. I forget at what point the sound pressure level will make your heart stop, but it was close. Go look it up if you care.

I took my pimped out blazer with its crazy sick sound system and rolled back and forth through Catawba's **ONE** intersection. Everyone knew who I was. You could see me and hear me coming from a mile away, not that there was much to get in the way. But still it was fun. All the kids loved me. I custom designed sound systems for lots of them. And all the parents hated what I was doing to their kids and their cars. I brought music to the frickin' town. Seriously I was Kevin Bacon. I was a big deal.

That was fun, for like two weeks.

And then I was bored again.

About the same time, my dad suddenly changed his rules and kicked me off my ass. He decided that I needed some structure and demanded I start going to school and get a job. The next year was probably the most labor-intensive time of my life. I was in school, I had two jobs and I mastered the art of playing pool.

I know what I said to you about school and how I hated it and everything and that I would never go to college. But once I was forced into taking college classes and realized that I could pick the courses I was interested in studying, well, then I actually kind of liked it. I mean it was a crappy little nothing school called Clark State Community College in Springfield, which was an annoying 90 minutes away from Catawba, but I liked it. I started with electrical engineering courses but when I realized that we would spend more time writing out designs and analyzing them than actually soldering shit, I lost interest and shifted gears. I enrolled in a religion course, a business course, a math course, and a business law course and I ended up doing pretty okay. I also ended up loving my business law classes and realize now, in hindsight, that it was incredibly valuable. I use the stuff I learned then pretty much every single day while I'm running my own company.

And the commute wasn't so bad because I had installed a CB radio in my truck. Even though I had that sick sound system that I loved, most of the time I would make the long drive in silence, listening to the random chatter over the CB radio. There weren't cell phones and GPS systems then to help drivers navigate their way. But if you had access to a CB radio you could get a hold of the truckers' conversation and all the information they passed back, like upcoming weather and traffic and construction and cops. Plus they talked all cool. They have their own lingo and if you listen long enough you can pick it up and sort of become a part of their gang. It was all, *"What's your 20? Just shot by the bear cave. Looked like 2 smokies and one miss piggy west bound. Rubber Duckie. 10-4."*

So cool.

My dad was a part of it, too. His factory wasn't far from my school and he had his own radio. If we were both in our trucks we'd pass information back and forth. It was nice, actually. We had our own handles for each other and I'm only telling you this because with all my cursing and cynicism and stuff, I feel like I owe you a little sentiment, alright? So anyhow, many years before the time in Ohio, my dad and I were in Indian Guides together. His name was Growling Bear and I was Howling Wolf. Back on the road we used those names again. It was kind of gay, but whatever.

When I wasn't in class or driving back and forth, then I was at one of my two jobs. In the mornings I worked as a back hoe operator at a construction site. It was a lot like Nintendo with the controller and it came easily to me. At nights I worked at a gas station. That wasn't brain surgery either. It was just work. I never worked so hard, before or after that—like sweaty, manual work. In that sense, Ohio was the toughest time in my life.

Every once in a while I would grab a drink with my dad. It didn't matter that I wasn't 21. In rural America, even in a really religious place like Catawba, a working man earns his drink. So, I did. But I didn't really like to just sit and drink. I liked to be doing something to keep my ADD mind occupied. That's why I started playing pool.

I never really played before I lived in Ohio but in that one year I got so good I was ranked as one of the top five players in the state. I shot so much pool it became totally natural to me. It was just like my NHL hockey days. I didn't have to think. I just saw the shots. I loved two rail bank shots. I loved hopping the balls. I made everything and I was a total show-off. I took important, tournament-winning shots with my eyes closed, just because I could. I only got better under pressure. And then there was Nine Ball, which I absolutely and completely fucking loved. That game is 100% about angles and strategy. It's fast and you have to be risky. It was perfect for me. I won every Nine Ball tournament I played. I hustled players all the time, just for fun.

People still ask me how I was so good. It's like that scene from *Catch Me If You Can* with Hanks and DiCaprio when Carl asks Frank how the hell he passed the bar exam in Louisiana. Sometimes people don't want to believe the simple truth. I was just awesome. All I did was play every second that I could and then I mastered it and won.

I played until I was the best and when I knew I couldn't get any better, well then I knew I was done and ready for next thing. I was done with pool and I was also done with Ohio. I had been there for more than a year.

The deal I made with my parents was that I'd stay away from Moline for at least two years, maybe longer if the crap hadn't settled down yet. But I couldn't make it that long. I'd already done everything I could in Ohio to stay sane. So, even if those guys were out there looking for me I decided I was going home. As it turned out, everyone was dead and gone. Someone way high up in Chicago had decided that the whole Moline crap was nonsense, I guess, and everyone who was involved suddenly "disappeared." The cops couldn't say where. I have a feeling a few of them ended up with a bullet of two in their heads, probably in the back of some car—one without the 22" Daytons. Obviously, I can't say for sure. It's the perfect wrap-up though so that's how I'm going to end the story, at least in my mind.

The thug dudes were dead in a trunk and I was alive and free to drive myself on home.

7

There Are Two Kinds of People
And I'm the Second

There's no honor in taking that after school job at Mickey Dee's.
Honor's in the dollar, kid.

-SETH DAVIS,

Boiler Room

Now that I'm a parent I realize how crazy hard it is to be one. IT'S SCARY SHIT! All you can hope for is that the decisions you make don't get your kid killed or leave them with any permanent scars.

Look, just circumcise your kid when he's a baby, okay? Get the doctor to do it early. I don't understand this new trend to leave that whole business natural. It's not more humane. You're just subjecting your kid to a life of insecurity and a messy situation to clean up. I say the best thing you can do for your kids is to cut off all the extra baggage early.

So I walked into the doctor's office to get a circumcision and of course there's about a gazillion authorization forms to fill out. Like I have time for that shit?!? Why medical records aren't electronic already, I have no idea. Anyway, I finally get to the last authorization form which was kind of funny. I called the nurse over to ask her about it and she was like, "Yeah. This one is just to give us authorization to send the excess skin to China so they can use it on kids born without eyelids." So it was really like a win/win situation. I could get my circumcision and then help out a bunch of Chinese kids, because I had a good amount of excess and all. The only issue is that—well—those kids almost always end up a little cockeyed.

Get it?

That was a joke. Yes, you get a joke in my book. I like jokes. This is my book. Laugh a little.

Back to business. Where was I? Um, I used to be really fat. I have major issues with religion. I have ADD. I'm bad at school. There was the thing about being a misfit. Then there was the thing in Daytona and then the shoot out and then Ohio. That gets us up to here.

I was nearly 21 and I moved back home to Moline with my mom. I got a job, this time without her help. It was at Best Buy. I don't want you to think I was, like, the stock boy or a checkout associate or anything less than the glorified god of the audio electronics department. You know how I'm a frickin' pro at that stuff. But it's not like you actually need to be an electronics wizard or an expert with customized audio systems fitted for solid gold Jeep Cherokees or Lamborghini Diablos or $400,000 Bentleys to work in audio electronics at Best Buy. Basically, you just need to be a good bull shitter who settles for making eight bucks an hour.

The eight bucks an hour really sucked. That's eight bucks BEFORE TAX, don't forget, so I couldn't help but look for a better angle to earn some extra cash. That's about when I heard about a little thing called the Employee Purchase Program, a perk that Best Buy decided to start for all the schmucks who have agreed to troll around the warehouse store for measly eight bucks an hour. The gist of this perk was that any Best Buy employee could purchase retail products at a price that was a mere 5% markup from the store's cost. If you know anything about the electronics industry—the audio electronics industry specifically—you know that the retail markup on all products is ludicrous.

On one particularly uneventful day in the audio department I was flipping through a product catalogue and I noticed the markup margin on one specific product was RIDICULOUSLY RETARDED. The listed retail price for this one pair of component speakers was $395. The employee purchase price was listed at just $75. I was like, "Holy crap!" There's a $320 difference between $395 and $75. I'm not asking you to work out complex equations here. It's arithmetic. On this one particular set of speakers, Best Buy was taking a huge profit margin. I couldn't help but think I should be able to grab a piece of the action.

It's not like I was looking for a way to screw Best Buy or anything. I had just been obsessed with this dope receiver, which through the Employee Purchase Program would cost me $200. But I didn't have $200 in my pocket. I was living with my mom and making less than eight bucks an hour, remember? And also, I really suck at saving money. I have never really learned how to do that. Being financially conservative is just NOT me. Luckily I have always been able to find a way to make a buck—even if I do spend it right after—so it all works out in the end, usually. In this case though, I was actually spending the money before I had even made it. I knew I could find some kind of angle. And then one day I came across the $395 speakers deal.

The next day I scraped together a little bit of cash and plunked down $75—the Employee Purchase cost for the ridiculously marked-up speakers. I was really loud about the whole purchase, telling everyone I worked with how I was buying these speakers as a "present" for my friend, Mario. He was a real guy and a friend of mine who had an obsession with cassette tapes. He had like two thousand, or something crazy. (It's really important to know what drives people—what they're passionate about. It can come in really handy. I'll go into that more, later.) Anyway, I knew I could get Mario to help me if he came out of the deal with more cassette tapes for his collection. I needed someone to help me test this angle I was knocking around in my head—I guess that's what you call an accomplice.

Here's how I thought it would work. Mario, who didn't work for Best Buy and wasn't eligible for Employee Purchase prices, simply had to return his new speakers to any Best Buy store. Since the speakers were "given to him as a gift" he wouldn't have a receipt to show. Without a receipt he would get a refund of $395 in store credit. The deal was that he would use $200 to buy me the receiver I wanted and then keep the remaining $195 in store credit to buy whatever he wanted (a shit ton more cassettes). That's how I thought it would work and that's exactly how it did work out.

Not bad for an original investment of $75, right? Well, Mario definitely thought so and was like, "LET'S DO IT AGAIN!!!"

Now Mario was a good guy and all, but what I quickly realized is that if the two of us repeated this over and over again, then it was kind of like stealing and we could eventually get caught. So I asked a couple of other friends to help me out, once each. And of course the whole thing worked perfectly every time. I wanted to be careful so I told them which stores to go to so we could spread things around. No one noticed a thing or ever asked a question. After a while, I realized that I didn't need anyone else to help me with that angle. I could do it solo. So I did.

In the end, I did that whole thing about fifty times. In fact, I did it until I had the sickest collection of home electronics and audio equipment you could possibly imagine.

Of course my store manager got a little suspicious once or twice but nothing ever came of it. I think it was amazing that he didn't catch on quicker. I mean, I bought the same pair of $75 speakers FIFTY different times. But technically I wasn't doing anything wrong. I was buying "gifts." It was a great lesson about simplicity and confidence. It was such a simple angle that is was impossible not to have confidence in it. And when my manager questioned me a handful of times, I always said with a hundred percent certainty, "It's such a good deal. They're all gifts for my friends." It was truly an amazing lack of central oversight that no one ever took the time to wonder if this one particular pair of speakers wasn't inappropriately priced under Best Buy's fabulous Employee Purchase Program pricing. All I can say is thank you Best Buy for having your head up your ass.

The Scooby Doo ending to this story is that I would've gotten away with it all if it hadn't been for my pesky fucking ego. Because, in my mind, figuring out something as great and easy as this just wouldn't be worth it if I couldn't talk about it.

You see, at the same time that I was running this speaker angle, Best Buy had initiated an undercover theft sting. It had nothing to do with me—I was small potatoes. I mean, granted my angle wasn't technically on the up and up. It was an "angle" after all and as you've learned, angles usually involve a little bending of the rules. But whatever, they weren't after me. Best Buy's real problem was much bigger than me and my speakers. Apparently, full trucks of merchandise were disappearing from time to time, costing Best Buy millions in stolen product. That kind of thing was way above me. The spies they sent in were looking for the crooked managers.

But first, the spy found me.

Actually, that's not really true. As it turned out, I found the spy first. I just didn't know he was a spy. I didn't know there were spies in play at all. I just thought he was a new employee who happened to be a cool guy so I befriended him. I don't know what to say. I like friends and, by the way, who would ever think that the masterminds who can't figure out their own pricing structures would be crafty enough to initiate a spy game?! In any case, we had a spy at our store and this spy became my legit friend and we hung out all the time. One night, after a few beers, I told the spy all about my speaker angle. I just couldn't keep my mouth shut any longer.

The next morning my phone rang at 5 am and my manager was barking at me to fill the first shift, unloading delivery trucks. This was really unfortunate because I only crawled into my bed at 4:30 am after partying all night at a friend's house. As I drove over to the store, digging the heel of my hand into my eyes, trying to rub the sleep out of them, I was just like, "Fuuuuuuuuuuuuuuuuuuuuuuuuuuuuuck." I was still drunk and all I knew was that I wanted to sleep—not unload a frickin' truck.

I walked in through the back of the store and met my manager in the middle of the warehouse. There weren't any trucks to unload but I was still drunk and I didn't notice at the time. He sent me into the storeroom to get something—I don't remember what. It wasn't important. That's not why he sent me. He sent me in because the cops were waiting for me— guns drawn and everything.

Talk about a shocker, when you're still drunk.

So it turned out that my angle cost Best Buy a little more than I had imagined. With that, I was arrested and charged with a felony because my "fraudulent activity" amounted to—well, it amounted to a lot. The cops took me to the station and dropped me into an interrogation room. I sat there and I waited, dripping with sweat, not because I was nervous but because it was like a hundred degrees in there and I was still drunk. I had so much Captain Morgan in me that I didn't know what was what. All I knew was that I was tired and I wanted to go to sleep.

Finally, around noon, this interrogator came into the room. This guy was a total badass. As he sat across from me he started to drill me with all sorts of carefully crafted questions. Before I knew it, he had me admitting to shit I never did and ratting out people I never even knew. I have no idea why, but for some reason this guy totally got into my head and scared the living shit out of me. To this day, no single person has scared me more than that dude. And all I wanted to do was get the hell out of that room and go to sleep. Anywhere. That's all I knew.

Felony or not, I just wanted to go to sleep.

By the time my mom bailed me out, I realized I had a real problem. I was charged with a felony and my case was going all the way to trial. And I had no lawyer, which was another problem. Add that to the fact that I had no money for a lawyer, which was a huge problem. So I went to my dad for a loan but he said no. One of his favorite parental policies was *if get yourself into it, you get yourself out of it.* I got myself into this one, for sure. But I also figured that there had to be some way to pull myself out and pay for it all.

When you're in major shit, the only way out is to move forward. I had to start somewhere so even though I couldn't pay for it I started looking for a lawyer. Actually I just grabbed the thick ass Yellow Pages and thumbed through it until I found the largest ad in the attorney section. I figured that if he could pay for that ad then he must have won at least a few cases. The guy's name was Michael McDermit. I called him up, told him my story and asked for a dollar amount for the kind of defense I would need. I wanted a flat fee—start to finish, with no BS.

He told me $2,800.

I could do that. I wasn't going to jail.

I got a loan against my 1988 Red Mustang LX, paid McDermit and we went to court. It was worth every penny. The judge ruled that—technically—I hadn't broken any laws. I bent them till they damn near snapped, but—technically—I hadn't broken a single law according to the fine print. I had never declared a value for the merchandise I got in the exchanges. That was crucial in the legal ruling. Because I always paid for the original $75 speakers, all I was doing was trading on the value Best Buy assigned to the speakers. Based on that, the judge declared that I was not guilty. My case was dismissed.

I hadn't done anything illegal. I just worked an angle.

As you can imagine, Best Buy was really pissed off. Not only did they lose their suit against me and all the merchandise I had collected, they had also been paying me unemployment throughout the proceedings. When I was declared not guilty, Best Buy was legally ordered to give me back pay for all the months since my wrongful termination. As an extra ass-whoop, the judge also ruled that Best Buy was responsible for reimbursing me for all my legal fees.

I will proudly admit that I'm an angler and a rule-bender, but I'm not a lazy sack of shit with an inflated sense of entitlement. I wasn't sitting on my ass throughout the proceedings hoping for anything beyond a not guilty verdict. The entire time I had another job, selling appliances at Montgomery Ward. But in the end, I came out of the whole ordeal a lot better than just, okay and not guilty. I got my $2800 back with interest and removed the loan against my car. I got my back pay. I still had thousands of dollars' worth of new electronic equipment and best of all, I WASN'T IN JAIL.

Honestly, I take credit for illustrating just how mismanaged Best Buy was. I don't know if they ever found the big manager thieves, but they did finally kill the Employee Purchase Program. And I will take full credit for that. So if you are a Best Buy troll who is still settling for eight bucks an hour, then I screwed you out of your one little perk. Sorry for that, but it might be time for you to find a new gig, anyhow.

I don't want to sit here and tell kids to steal or take advantage of people or anything like that. I just happened to see a loophole in the way things were supposed to operate. I took it and it happened to work out for me. I'm just saying that if you see an angle and you take action on it aggressively, then it might work out for you too. If you are willing to do what others are willing not to do, then you can come out on top. Be a little bit creative if you want to make more than eight bucks an hour. The opportunities are there. That's all I'm saying.

As I see it, there are two types of people in this world. First there are the people who want to be on a track. They want to put in their hours, follow the rules and get a paycheck. And there's absolutely nothing wrong with that if that is how you are wired, although I hope you are earning *at least* ten bucks an hour. There are *those* type of people in this world and then there are *the others*. They're the people who see a cookie cutter life as the ultimate imprisonment—the death of creativity, a hopeless track to never get where you want and what you deserve. That's definitely me. I'm that kind of guy.

And I'm in good company.

I don't mean any disrespect to Steve Jobs, especially since he isn't with us any longer to defend himself. And I definitely don't want to piss off Bill Gates in the off-chance that he's interested in setting up a personalized educational fund for my two girls, but both of those guys were shady. They were far shadier than I ever was, if we have to draw comparisons, and to date, they have also been more successful. See the correlation yet? In Gates case, he sold an operating system to IBM before it even existed. He didn't even have any idea that he could (or would) build it when he took the money. And Jobs completely robbed Xerox of their prototype by asking to "borrow" it for a second. He completely ripped it off and that's what became the Mac operating system—the foundation of the Mac as we still know it. Donald Trump, the MySpace founders, Zuckerberg—you name it, every company I can think of was built by people who didn't play by the rules. They all saw an angle, took a risk and were willing to do what others were not.

You read about those guys as icons who sit in their Ivory Towers and can do no wrong, but even Warren Buffett started out by running around Omaha hustling people all the time. It's just the way the world works if your eyes are open and you look. That doesn't make it right or less scary, but it IS true.

At the end of the Best Buy ordeal, I was extremely grateful that I wasn't convicted of a felony. But at that time I also realized that I was (and still am) the kind of guy that needs to really be free to go after it.

It's scary to be off of any chartered path, but it's also fun. It's the most true and honest way I know how to be. If I go out and kill it for Best

Buy by selling six completely pimped-out audio systems in one afternoon then Best Buy has an awesome day and I still take home my eight bucks an hour. I don't think you can ever get ahead in a space like that. But if I own my own company and I sell 5,000 subscriptions to Time Life, well then, that pay-out is all for me.

I love to run and gun. I call it "sticking your pecker out there" because it's scary, makes you vulnerable and, hell, it can get chopped off—and not just in a circumcision kind of way. Castration is scary shit. I get it. No one wants to lose it all. But the thing is if you don't push yourself, especially when you're scared, then you'll never be the guy who makes it. You have to stick your pecker out there to know what you can really do.

8
Welcome to the Internet, Danny LaRusso

Man who catch fly with chopstick, accomplish anything.

-MR. MIYAGI,

The Karate Kid

Actually, a million times out of ten I am grabbing the flyswatter. Forget the dumb chopsticks. I'm not wasting an entire day on one fucking fly. I'll end it as nature intended—with a flyswatter. Just as soon as I'm done with that I will spend the next three days—without interruption—creating a mechanized system built to swat-annihilate every fly as it enters my world so that I never have to waste my time on any of this fly business ever again.

But I do like the chopstick sentiment about accomplishing something nearly impossible, especially if it's something that everyone else thinks is basically retarded or insane. And I like the movie, *Karate Kid*. In general, movies are awesome. If they make this book into a movie I can guarantee you that it will totally kill. It will be better than the book simply because movies are better than books. Just think how you'll get *to actually see* the craziness in my head instead of just having to take my word for it. I'll make sure that the art director perfectly captures the little ninjas in my head fighting death duels with samurai swords and nuclear bombs all against the backdrop of my fifth grade teacher talking on and on about Louis and Clark or some shit. It will be so awesome. Seriously, I hope that this book doesn't ruin the movie for you in the way that books can do that. I'm serious.

Yes, it's true that I don't read a lot of books and you're probably remembering right now that earlier I admitted to never actually reading a full book from start to end. That doesn't affect my argument. The point is still the same. I'm always warning the people who sit around with their noses crammed up inside a book to be careful. "Don't let the book ruin the movie for you." That's my thing. It's true and it's worth remembering, because it happens all the time.

Just wait until the next Nicholas Sparks' book-movie is released and all the girls are bitching and moaning that it just wasn't the same as the book. If you didn't read the book, you'd be all, "It wasn't so bad, for a chick flick. Good cinematography, at least. And there was that one tits scene too." And instead of getting points for taking your date to the chick flick and chalking it up to two hours of mindless entertainment away from the stress of your life and job, now you're stuck wasting the rest of the night listening to your date rattle off a very long list of reasons why the movie just wasn't as good as the book. At this point, you know it's best to just give up on the night because you're absolutely, never going to get laid. And in that case, the book ruined a lot more than just the movie for you.

Movies should be enjoyed for what they are: entertainment. I don't like reading books because my head is a trippy place. Not only can I not focus well enough so that the words in each sentence become an idea that follows the last—I can't quiet the ideas that are already in my head long enough to make space for a book's ideas. I can, however, focus on a movie. I focus on them for entertainment or for a much-needed vacation from my head. Because when the lights go down in a movie theatre, it's one of the few times in life that my mind switches off, or at least shuts down some of its firing zones. I love movies because they get me *out* of my head.

When we make the movie version of my story, I'm not sure how the next part fits in. Maybe it will be some sort of stage aside where I talk into the camera only for the benefit of the theatre audience. We'll figure that out later, I'm sure. But since you are, in fact, reading this book right now, I want to give you a little value add—my killer list of the ten all-time best movies in my book (*ahem, literally*).

Then we can get back to the point of this chapter (which is how I discovered the Internet and learned how to kick its ass Karate Kid style via the wax-on-wax-off method of learning). So here it goes:

Shoemoney's Top Ten Movies

(Which are a thousand times better than the hack list that Quentin Tarantino might throw at you.)

1. *Iron Man 1 and 2.* Okay. Seriously. Who doesn't want to be Tony Stark? Not only is he a superhero, but you take away the superhero suit and he's still a genius, billionaire, playboy, philanthropist. Nice. I love him, but not in a gay way. (*Here I am using the term "gay" to mean same-sex preference and not as I defined it earlier.*)

2. *Megamind.* Yes, this is a cartoon. Get over it or else you will miss a fan-fucking-tastic film. It's Will Ferrell. It's witty, adult banter that you won't care if your kids recite word for word forever, just like mine do. Also I'm adding it not only because I am a dad but because I would like you to know that I am incredibly well-diversified in the culture I consume. Don't expect just high-budget action movies here.

3. *Blow.* An outlaw entrepreneur takes you for a ride and makes you believe that you are every bit capable of being a high-fashioned drug lord. Plus, you will learn a thing or two about exactly what not to do when you're starting out as a drug smuggler and also once you've "made it" in drug society. The lessons from this movie work in any industry and social circle, which is a bonus.

4. *Great Expectations.* I told you I'm diversified, folks. I give Charles Dickens and Ethan Hawke equal credit for that line I love, which began this whole thing. "I'm not going to tell it how it happened. I'm going to tell it how I remember it." It's brilliant and fucking universal. This life we are all living is all about how we see it, how we angle within it, and then ultimately how we are remembered by someone else. I see myself as Pip. At first he doesn't expect much from his life. Eventually his view changes, but he has to battle against everyone else's low expectations of him. All the while, he never really expects that he won't get what he really wants—the girl. Deep. I know.

5. *Forrest Gump.* Classic underdog story. It's brilliant. Here you see the impact that one person can have on the era when that's the last thing he ever plans to do. There's a moral about ignorance and innocence here. Go figure it out but don't ever quote that line to me. (We've been over that.)

6. *Old School.* I know that I am not the first guy to say that this movie is about me and I don't care. This movie is about me. I AM ONE OF THOSE GUYS. I live in a college town and I am constantly plotting the frat that I will start for myself and the guys in college who are still nerds. Except my fraternity would be so completely awesome because we would have even more capital to play with than Speaker City could ever sponsor. Also, I already know the dean so we wouldn't waste time with any of that hassle. This is honestly on my list of things to do. Let me know if you want to pledge.

7. *The Pursuit of Happyness.* This is about the only movie that really gets to me, way down, emotionally. It doesn't make me cry (because I don't cry and I'll get to that story in a few chapters). But still it really moves me. Just when I start to think that I have it rough, I watch this and I'm all *holy shit.* That's what I mean about movies. The right ones can really get to you and move you. They help you relate to other possibilities and

people. This movie will teach you what it means to have a hard life. Also, they get that some people just don't know how to spell long words and it's not a big deal.

8. *The Lincoln Lawyer.* For my money, it doesn't get any more psychologically thrilling than this. I watch this movie at least once every year just to fuck with myself a little.

9. *Freakanomics.* I didn't add this to my list just to sound incredibly well-diversified. This documentary is truly fascinating. It unravels the shit that really makes people tick; that never gets old.

10. *Iron Man 1 & 2.* I started this list with a double whammy which is technically two films. I agreed to give you TEN must-watch movies, and I did that, didn't I? You can thank me later for these suggestions once you've had a chance to check all of them out. In the meantime, let's get back to the focus of the chapter.

I read somewhere that every day of your life you're getting better *at something.*

No, I'm not lying to you here or trying to be ironic. I did actually *read* it somewhere, just not in a book that I was reading cover to cover. It was probably somewhere online, okay? I just hope that the person who came up with this isn't reading my book someday and is all, "I'm suing that thieving asshole." And if you did come up with that line and are reading my book, I can tell you that I'm not trying to steal your line. I don't do that. I have enough lines of my own and if you do come forward with proof that this is your line, then in the second edition (and more importantly in the movie version of this story) you will get due credit. I have to leave this quote in here because it's an important thought that has really influenced how I see my life.

I'm on a tangent, again. I'm aware.

I read somewhere that [insert wise person's name here] said that every day of your life you're getting better at something. And I totally agree. If you spend all day trying to catch a fly with chopsticks, you'll be getting better at that. If you spend seven hours a day riding a bike, you'll get better at it. That stuff is obvious. What's really worth recognizing is that this same idea holds true for the stuff you're doing unintentionally or mindlessly. For example, if you're unemployed, every day you're without a job, you are getting better at being unemployed. If you're constantly lying to your boss and weaseling out of situations, then you're constantly getting better at that skill set. If you sit in a lumpy, awkward chair that slumps you over a desk and a computer while you ignore your constantly ringing phone, then every day you're getting better at slumping over your computer and zoning out your phone. It's that simple. But it can be a crazy powerful motivational factor to, at least, think about how you're spending your time and what you're intentionally (and unintentionally) getting better at.

I don't know if hearing this idea years ago would have made much of a difference in the decisions that I made about how I spent my time each day. It does, however, make for a really gratifying review of all the dead-end, completely unimpressive jobs that I have held over the years. If I look at each one, I realize that even in the time I was wasting or screwing off at Happy Joe's or Eagle's Grocery or Sound Advice or Best Buy or Montgomery Ward or Target or Sears, I was actually getting better, every single day, at a skill that I use and rely on to run the business that I own today.

After a few months of slicing pizzas at Happy Joes, I realized that money was good and I wanted more of it. Genius, right? I wasn't spending any time doing homework, which left every afternoon and evening free. I decided to take a second job at the local grocery store bagging groceries, which I soon learned was a completely miserable job (mostly because the manager was a little shit). But the hourly pay was better than Happy Joe's by two bucks, so I stayed and put up with it. Since I'm not really great at putting up with lip from customers and little shit managers, I started to find ways to make the job a little less miserable. At night when it wasn't busy, I would grab another guy and we'd use the frozen foods aisle to bowl a few rounds with frozen turkeys and 2 liter pops. Or sometimes we'd use the giant trash compactors in the warehouse to practice field goal kicks with paper towels. We'd play, sometimes for an hour, until I'd hear, "Jeremy, to the bakery for cleanup" over the PA. Then I would head over to mop up spilled orange juice. It was crazy and irresponsible and I got really good at inventing ways to make seven hour shifts of bagging crabby people's pork chops and I Can't Believe It's Not Butter, actually fun.

Besides learning to recognize the wastoid business methods of a drug dealing boss and dodging bullets underneath cars, my work at Sound Advice was pretty straight forward. I spent all my time there getting really good at everything that had to do with audio dynamics. And that expertise helped me build custom audio systems as a side job while I was exiled in Ohio. It got my foot into the door at Best Buy, and lent to a ridiculously dense knowledge of everything electrical.

The time I spent on the floor at Best Buy was also really valuable because that was when I started practicing sales tactics. I used everything I knew about automotive electronics to tell my customers stories about the car that they could have if they bought all this extra shit. I learned how to size up a person and give him the perfect pitch. I learned that the story always sells the product—that people buy shit when they believe it will make them better or happier. It's that simple. I understood that right away.

In sales and marketing, understanding your audience is the most important thing. Actually, it's way more important than anything you know about the product you are selling. I sold washers and dryers at Montgomery Ward and Sears. I knew a lot about electronics and none of that knowledge helped me a lick. I got into the heads of my suburban customers and I knew what they wanted. They wanted reliability. They wanted to know that they were buying something to make their lives easier. I understood this and that was the reason I was so damn good at selling washers and dryers. I also learned about the upsell—or what I dubbed—"The Cheese." Basically, it's the extended warranty.

The average customer at Sears bought an extended warranty with their appliance 15% of the time. My customer's bought them 40% of the time because I understood that my buyers were purchasing reliability and ease. They almost wanted the warranty MORE than the washer and dryer. It was a no-brainer. The first time my store manager saw that my "Cheese" sales rate was 40%, he called me into his office. Sears started sending me out to all the neighboring stores to teach the other numbskulls what the hell I was doing. So I did. And I got better. I was notorious at Sears all because I understood that the story sells the product and I'm a damn good story teller, if you haven't noticed.

Which is how Kristine found me, I guess. I haven't ever been an easy guy to miss once you're looking for me, but I never found out how she knew who I was in the first place. She just showed up one day as I was about to close another Maytag LAT8600 with The Cheese.

She walked right up to me and asked, "Are you Jeremy Schoemaker?"

And I was like, "Yes."

And she said, "I hear you're good at Macs. Are you good with Macintoshes?"

And I was like, "Yes. If by "good" you mean, I play a lot of games on Macs, then—yes."

Now remember, this was back in 1995 and Macs weren't exactly the sexy, mainstream things that we know today. In lots of ways they were actually kind of clunky, but I just always preferred them to IBMs so that's what I used to play all my games. Now, it wasn't like I had ever taken a class or read a manual about them or anything, I was just really frickin' good at gaming on them. So that's exactly what I told her, but she wasn't even fazed.

Kristine was starting an ISP—an Internet Service Provider. She explained that it would be like a local version of AOL, a place for people to get online. Her problem was that she didn't have anyone on staff that knew anything about Macs which also meant they couldn't do any customer support for the growing clientele of Mac users. She needed me. She needed a Mac guy.

So here she was, in Sears, handing me her card and offering me a job on the spot. She just wanted me to say, "Yes, I'm that guy." I never thought for a second that I couldn't do it, but I don't make a habit of over-promising anything. She offered to pay me double whatever I was making there at Sears if I would just say yes and start the next day.

I had no problem changing jobs. It wasn't like I was loyal to Sears or anything. I'm a cowboy, anyhow. I like a new challenge so I was totally ready to go join up with her. I just really wanted her to understand that I was a gamer. So I told her again, that when I said I was good, I meant I played a lot of games on Macs.

She was like, "Whatever." She told me where to show up the next day and took off.

No matter what the job, I've learned something valuable in each situation. Every single one. Even in the two days I worked at Target, I learned something. They hired me to be an electronics guy and then they had me stocking cat food. My job was to make sure that all the labels matched up perfectly on the shelf. Seriously. Right then I learned that some things aren't even worth the time it takes to bitch about them. I walked out of that job without telling anyone anything or getting my paycheck. That was the smartest thing I could have done. You have to consider what your time is worth.

After Kristine left I thought about her offer for exactly twenty minutes. It seemed like a good thing to do. I knew, at the very least, I would learn something new and that would be worth my time. So, I quit Sears right then, like literally twenty minutes after Kristine left and I had made up my mind. I wasn't going to waste the rest of the day working when I could be home playing video games. That's just me. Like I said, I'm a cowboy. I don't give a shit.

I knew that I would learn something at Kristine's shop, Internet Express. I just didn't know that working there would be world changing for me. That's exactly what it turned out to be. I learned more valuable skills in that time than in any other single experience of my life. Internet Express was like my Karate Kid. I learned everything through practical applications and my timing, in the bigger context of the world, was perfect.

At first Internet Express was a small operation. There were only four of us. Even though I was there to be the Mac guy, I was also in charge of configuring all the user accounts. I would go into the black screen interface and enter the commands and look at this file and that file. *Wax-on-wax-off.* What I didn't know was what I was actually doing was learning the Linux operating system. That's the backbone of every server.

I learned virtual web hosting and DNS. Before I knew it, I was a black belt wizard at Linux administration. I could control a server from start to finish and sideways, even. I knew how to compile and program and everything that you had to do. The only thing I struggled with was some of the graphics. I wanted to know how to manipulate graphics for icons and mouse-overs or anything else I might need. Since I knew that would be tough to teach myself, I found a Photoshop class at the community college and enrolled. Eventually I had a complete tool set. I completely re-did Internet Express' website just for fun.

That was just about the time that this gay model came into the shop, looking to create a personal website. He wanted to include a bunch of nudes, which made Kristine nervous. I pulled her aside and asked if she would be okay with me taking on the project for myself, on the side.

And she was all, "Whatever." So I did. I created an awesome website for the gay model dude—because I could. And then I knew HTML, too.

I can't say that I knew it in the moment, but looking backwards, it's totally clear. My experience at Internet Express definitely set me up for success. I took a cowboy gamble and was willing to do what others were willing not to and once again, it paid off. My success also had to do with me, always finding ways to get better at what I was inherently good at and what I enjoyed.

And that, my friends, is how I discovered the Internet and became master of that universe.

9
How to Live in a Cave

If you are deliberately trying to create a future that feels safe, you will willfully ignore the future that is likely.

-SETH GODIN,

Linchpin: Are You Indispensable?

I hope you're not expecting me to talk about something woodsy here. You should know me better than that by now. I'm just not an outside kind of dude. I would much rather spend my time in the penthouse at the Palms or having lunch at Chateau Marmont. Shit, this whole chapter should be about what happens in the Grotto. That's a cool cave. That's the kind of outdoors I like.

I definitely do not like camping. I don't like the bugs or sleeping on the ground. I don't like being so cold at night that you think your nuts might actually freeze and fall off. I don't like singing Kumbaya around the fire. S'mores are good though. I am good with the S'mores, but nothing else. I know because I tried to like it once, for a few nights at stay-away camp when I was13. I stayed for two days before I had enough. When I have enough—well then, I'm just done. That pretty much goes for anything. The rule definitely stands for camping. I had enough. I was done. So I ran away.

The cool way do it would have been to disappear in the night with a girl. I tried that. I asked a few, but they all said no. Whatever. None of the girls wanted to give fatty a piece in the woods. They're loss. So instead I got two guys to go with me. The three of us gathered a handful of things like blankets and pretzels and that was about the extent of our escape plan.

We left in the middle of the night and just started to walk through the woods in the middle of nowhere, Iowa. We walked for what seemed like forever. We stopped once to eat our pretzels and then we kept walking. I don't know if you've ever run away from camp or had any other reason to be walking aimlessly through the woods in the middle of the night, but I can tell you that it's really dark and it's really scary. There are all these creepy noises that set you on edge. Plus we had zero clue where we were headed. I'm not embarrassed to say that I was scared. I wasn't like piss my pants freaked—I was just a little scared. So when I spotted a farm house—the only sign of life that we saw for five hours—I decided that we were turning ourselves in.

That family turned out to be really cool. I guess they could have been twisted fucks living out there in the middle of nowhere, but they weren't. They were very nice and even gave us breakfast while we waited for our parents to come get us. None of them were very cool when they finally showed up. Whatever. The escape mission was a success. I got out of the frickin' woods and back to normal life which gets us back to the point of this story: my cave.

Side Note: Since I already brought up the Grotto a few pages ago, let me quickly tell you now so that I don't forget to tell somewhere in this book. IF YOU EVER HAVE THE CHANCE TO GO TO THE PLAYBOY MANSION, YOU SHOULD GET YOUR ASS THERE! That place is amazing. I don't know what it does to people, but you're pretty much in awe the whole time. You feel crazy, like you're willing to jump in the pool naked or snort lines off a bunny's tits. It's about a hundred times cooler than you ever think it could be. Before you know it, Ron Jeremy shows up and you punch him in the face just so you can say that you punched Ron Jeremy in the face. Okay, that last part didn't happen, but it could have. I totally would have done it.

A few months ago I saw Brad Pitt when I was having lunch at Chateau Marmont. I had a whole plan in my head about how I was going to punch him in the face when he walked past our table. Then I'd get arrested. I might even get slapped with a lawsuit or a restraining order. Can you imagine the publicity?! That shit would be all over TMZ. You can't buy that type of exposure. I'd even counter-sue Pitt, too. You're missing the point if you're wondering what the hell I'd sue him for after I punched him in the face. You don't have to have a legitimate reason to sue someone. You can just sue. I'd just do it for the headlines and then I'd withdraw it. I really thought the whole idea was genius. He never walked past our table, though, so it was all no dice. But can you imagine if he did?! That's the kind of stuff I mean when I say that I'm willing to do what others are willing not to do. I would totally be willing to punch Brad Pitt or Ron Jeremy in the face for the exposure. It would be awesome.

Look, I never said that I was normal. I'm pretty sure my brain doesn't exactly work like normal people's work. That's the other point I've been trying to get to before I can tell you my cave story. I have a crazy brain that is filled with insane anxiety.

Basic anxiety is really just the fear that something bad is going to happen to you, like you sleep through your alarm when you need to be up extra early or you don't hook the lock correctly in a public bathroom stall and the door swings open to a line of waiting dudes as you're bent over wiping your ass. That's basic anxiety. Extreme anxiety is when you have constant irrational fear in your head.

I think I was just born with a crazy brain and a lot of anxiety. That explains a lot of it. But a ton of crazy stuff happened to me too, which has only made my anxiety even worse.

I am not going to go into the details, but if you're going to get me then you really need to have a complete picture of my world. So I have to mention that I was actually abused when I was really little. That left a big scar, which I had to deal with when I was all grown up. I fantasized for a long time about finding that guy from my old neighborhood, driving over to his house and killing him. At one point I even knew where he lived. I'm not exactly sure what would happen if I just ran into him one day. I guess I hope that I don't. So that left a scar, for sure, and probably had a lot to do with the irrational fear and anxiety, which plagued me for many years. I was also really pissed at my parents about the whole thing. I have never understood how they could let that happen or that they would never address it and try to fix it. To this day, they still go on thinking that I was too young to remember.

I wasn't.

So there was that abuse thing at the very beginning and then there was a crazy string of deaths in my life. My uncle overdosed on drugs. One of my aunts committed suicide and then the other one died of cancer. Then my great aunt passed away and finally my grandpa died too. At that point, my dad's entire side of the family—everyone except my grandma—was gone. During that death span, I saw my cousins more at funerals than holidays and celebrations. The world completely stopped making sense. It wasn't true that people got to live. Instead I started to see life being all about death.

I got completely fixated on death in a way that only a guy with tunnel vision can.

Happy, happy, joy, joy---death, death, death.

I couldn't sleep. I would stay up all night because I was convinced that nuclear war was about to begin, any second. I also had a hard time with traffic and moving cars. I was sure that any minute I was about to get hit. I also started researching all these different types of poison and became convinced that they were getting into my system somehow. I thought my drinks were poisoned and my food was poisoned. I thought someone was after me. It was a conspiracy. I'd just be sitting in class and out of nowhere I would start having a full-on panic attack, with all the sweating and panting and everything. And oh yeah, I thought the building was going to explode.

Eventually, somehow, it got better—mostly because I got old enough to self-medicate, usually with alcohol.

Fast forward to Internet Express. I was 22.

I would say that I was happy then. I was totally obsessed with mastering programming and my brain was occupied. And then one day I met up with my best friend. We were headed to the mall to buy beepers. I noticed he had this weird limp. He explained that it was probably because he played golf the day before and he was out of shape. Like a dick I said, "It's probably cancer." Well, maybe I shouldn't have been such a dick because it turned out that it was cancer.

Bone cancer is extremely rare and it's basically un-fucking-heard-of in young guys. But my buddy got it and six months after the day we bought our pagers together I was at his funeral. That started another insane string of deaths. Three days later a different friend hung himself in his front yard. He came from a really dysfunctional family and had a bad cocaine problem for a long time. Anyhow, one night he did too much and he ended up hanging himself from the tree in his front yard. His house was right at the corner of one of the busiest intersections in our town so a bunch of people saw him dangling before the cops got there to clean it all up. He said in a letter that he wanted his mom to come home all fucked up and find him like that. It was a mess. Then Tupac and Biggie and Kurt Cobain all died and again, the world did not make any sense to me.

Anxiety set in hard after that.

I was 400 pounds at the time and I smoked like a chimney. I easily went through two packs of Newports a day. I was so jittery I didn't even try to hide it. I couldn't sit still. I had all these really crazy ideas running through my head: *Should I get into my car and run into another car? How should I do it? Which road should I do it on? Maybe I should cut off the tip of my nose. Maybe I should slice my cheek open or stick a fork in my eye. Maybe I should saw off my dog's head. Maybe I should set the house on fire.* First I thought about all this insane shit and then I started telling everyone around me all the insane shit I was thinking. That's when things got even weirder.

When you say the craziest thing you can think of out loud, to your friends, you would think they'd be all, "Whoa dude. You're messed up." But that wasn't what happened. It was the exact opposite. I would be like, "Man, I'm thinking about cutting my off my dog's head." And then my friend would be like, "I know. Right? Like an hour ago I had this guy's dick in my mouth and I was thinking about biting it." And then I'd be like, "Whoa. We're all fucked up and we're all just going to end up ripping each other's faces off and when did you get gay?" And then another friend would be like, "Is it weird that I think about my mom when I jerk off?" Around and around we went like that. It was all totally warped.

I mean, people are really twisted. Maybe it's not just me, after all.

Finally I went to our family doctor for some help. He didn't really take me seriously, especially since he was off for vacation the very next day. He wrote me a script for Prozac and patted me on the back. At the time Prozac was pretty much the national drug of America. Doctors were handing it out like candy. But in the time since then we have learned, through a lot of research and some really unfortunate suicides, that Prozac can actually increase anxiety in some people.

The second day I was on Prozac my blood pressure sky-rocketed. I literally could not sit still and the crazy thoughts only intensified. I was a 400-pound crazy person, pacing around in circles and muttering about how the stray cats were coming to kill us all, which would be the final straw and then I would have no choice but to finally to saw off my dog's head. My heart felt like it was going to pound itself right out of my chest. I stopped sleeping completely.

My insomnia lasted for three whole days, after which, my parents finally took me to the hospital. Thank [insert your deity here] they did!

They left me alone in the examining room and made me promise to tell the doctor everything. I agreed but I was like, *"That's it for me. They're totally taking me to the asylum."* I told the doctor every crazy thing that had happened and that I had thought. He told me to get off Prozac immediately. They swapped my meds for Xanax and sent me home.

I felt better, almost immediately. I could actually sit down and be still. I could really lay down on a couch and rest. The world started to come back into focus a little bit at a time. Once I got my bearings I knew I had to make some kind of change.

One thing I took away from my exile in Ohio was that I actually enjoyed school when I was learning about topics that interested me. My mom still had not given up her dream that I would make it to college and a bunch of my childhood friends were at Western Illinois University. I visited them a few times and the place just fit me. So after surviving my first massive psychological breakdown I decided to go back to school. My mom was over the moon, ridiculously happy. Despite any money problems we had, my parents agreed to pay my tuition as well as provide me with a small "allowance" for food and basics.

I call it college, but actually it was a lot more like 13th grade. I didn't have the grades to get into Western so I started, Rudy Ruettiger-style, at the community college. I wasn't there for a degree so I didn't care where my actual classes were held. I just wanted to hang out, lay low, push away the real world and become obsessed with something abstract and interesting. For two and a half years I cherry picked classes at Spoon River Community College. I never met with an advisor or mapped out a degree path. I took computer science, political science, criminal law, religion and debate. I went to all of them because I was really interested. I didn't care about passing or failing because the credits were absolutely pointless to me. I just wanted to learn. I have to say, it was awesome.

Debate is what really captured me though. Partly it was because one of my roommates was a national champion debater and we'd practice a couple times a week. I've always been pretty good off-the-cuff, but I really liked the format of the whole practice. I absolutely loved giving up all of my best stuff on one side and then having to flip, instantly, and re-strategize for the opposite point. I couldn't get enough of it. I'm a naturally gifted asshole, what can I say? I was perfectly suited to be a great debater—another God-given talent. For about a half of a second I even contemplated law school. But that only lasted, literally, a half of a second. I wasn't ready for big plans like that yet.

We literally lived in an Animal House—nine guys in a falling-down three-story house who wanted to screw around as much as possible. Most of the time we would get completely wasted and invent games to play, which always took place on the roof. We played roof golf, driving balls onto different corners of campus. We'd also steal balls from the bowling alley and roll them off the roof in a bowling shoot out. It was probably the most fun part of my life. And the fun was well-deserved and perfectly timed.

ADD Side Note (especially for college kids): Like I told you before, I got a small food allowance from my parents each month. But anyone who went away to college knows that alcohol becomes a higher priority than food. So, obviously, I spent my food allowance on alcohol and mostly lived off of Ramen Noodles. But that can get old real quick if you don't have something to spice it up with, like say, the Colonel's glorious eleven herbs and spices from KFC. But that could be quite a splurge, given my measly little budget. I had to find a way to really make a few bucks count. We started going to the buffet every once in a while, investing the $4.99 for mounds of potatoes and piles of biscuits and, of course, tons of chicken. But even I couldn't eat it all. So I started bringing my own doggie bags and stuffed enough chicken into the gallon Ziploc bags to last me a few extra days. That's how you eat like a king when you're college ass is broke. I highly recommend it if those buffets still exist, just don't forget your Ziplocs and a gym bag or something, to carry out thirty bucks of herby, spicy goodness, discreetly.

Going to classes, practicing debate, fucking around like assholes on a dangerous roof—that's mostly how I spent my days at Western in the beginning. But as the months wore on, I started to spend more and more time alone, holed up in my basement bedroom. That was my cave. Even though I can be a major extrovert, cracking jokes and being loud, my natural tendency is to be alone. I love to sit in the dark to recharge. My cave was perfect for this.

I had a bed, my stereo equipment, a computer and a DSL line and that was pretty much all I needed. Over the next two years the empty space of the room filled up with piles of dirty clothes, old takeout containers, and crusty Ramen cups. I didn't really notice.

If you love being online, you can become a recluse without even realizing it. My parents were sending me a few bucks a month, which basically covered the cost of my alcohol, Ramen Noodles, and KFC stockpiles, but I wanted money beyond that so I leveraged all the skills I learned at Internet Express to start freelance web designing. I got a ton of business quickly because I would undercut all the competition (which wasn't much). I was doing beautiful websites, front to back, for like 200 bucks. The sites even had shopping carts way before anyone knew how to design shopping carts. This was back in the pre-PayPal era when online transactions used X.com. That's how I supported myself and how I began to justify being online pretty much every second of the day.

I loved to dick around in chat rooms. I would always be the administrator, though, because I wanted to be the one to control the conversations and everything. Most people had totally lame handles like jack@aol.com. Not me. I started picking up domains just so I could have a bunch of different handles like Jeremy@isapimp.com or whatever the latest meme was. It was super easy to do and I thought it was hilarious.

At the time there was only one company regulating domain ownership and the process was completely lax. You were allowed to go in and register any domain you could think of and you could hold it legitimately, without payment, for 90 days. If you didn't pay for it within that time your ownership would lapse, but then you just had to go back and immediately re-register it for another 90 days. I did this with a ton of domains, stuff like baseballcards.com; mensshoes.com; dipshit.com; macgamer.com; and shoemoney.edu. You also didn't have to prove accreditation at the time to hold an edu and I had a lot of fun with that. I collected psychosis.edu and pimp.edu. When the regulations got more serious I eventually dumped them all. I sold a few for basically nothing. In retrospect, I should have kept them, especially shoemoney.edu and macgamer.com. Those would be gold mines today. But I wasn't doing it for the money. I was just having fun.

Whatever time I had left in the day I spent playing Quake and writing cracks and hacks.

This is officially where we enter the tech-geek part of the chapter, just so you know.

You need to understand how revolutionary Quake was. It was one of the first multi-player games, meaning players all in different parts of the house, the country, or the world could connect through the server and meet in shoot-out death duels within different levels of a futuristic world. Trent Reznor designed the sound and audio and you could get these nail guns with the NIN logo on them to use as your weapon. You could jump and move and hop around like a super-human ninja with a gun. I was obsessed. Eventually I started to play competitively.

The thing about me and games, if you remember, is that I don't really like playing anything unless I can find a way to cheat. I have to be able to find an angle. That's just the way I work—the way I see the world, virtually and in reality. So I completely dissembled the game, programmatically, figured out how it worked and then I knew where the shortcuts were. And I would win—not because I was the best, but because I could always find a quicker way to the end.

Like I told you (and Kristine), I've always been a Macintosh user. Now the only problem with Quake was that the originating software company, ID Software, didn't create an official Mac version of the game. Someone like me (but not me) took this as an opportunity and completely re-wrote the code to support the Mac and made the Mac client. But because ID Software didn't support the ripped-off version, there was no place for users to go to get help or trouble-shooting advice. I understood the whole system, its code, and I could design and support a website. With all those tools I launched my first big site: macquake.com. I had a crap load of traffic right from the start. Anyone could come to the site if they needed help, like to figure out what to do when the interface wouldn't load or to understand how to use a map within a certain level.

That's when I pretty much forgot about all the waking life going on around me, outside my cave.

Every once in a while the guys upstairs would get pissed that I was tying up the phone line for hours on end with my dial-up connection (Remember that??) and they'd do something really jack-ass to get my attention and piss me off. One night they jumped up and down, again and again, on the floor just above my room. They pounded the wooden floor so hard that the vibration shattered my ceiling lamp. With all 400 of my pounds I stomped up the stairs, flipped over the couch and started wailing on one of them. I didn't like being disturbed.

Anyhow, that's basically how you live in a cave. You just need the Internet, crap loads of Ramen Noodles, and a real love for solitude.

10
Take the Blue Pill

Imagination is more important that knowledge.

-ALBERT EINSTEIN

When anyone starts working for me I always tell them the same, first thing. I tell them that they really should take the blue pill because once they know what I know, there's no going back.

Please tell me that you have seen *The Matrix*. There's that one scene right before Neo sees what the matrix actually is when he is sitting with Morpheus in those big arm chairs. Neo doesn't know exactly what is wrong; he just senses that the world isn't quite right. And Morpheus has the answers. It's all right there in front of him to take. He just has to choose a pill—the red one or the blue one.

Morpheus says, "I imagine you're feeling a little bit like Alice tumbling down the rabbit hole…You have the look of a man who accepts what he sees because he expects to wake up…Take the blue pill and the story ends. You will wake up in your bed and believe whatever you want to believe. Take the red pill and you stay in Wonderland and see how deep the rabbit hole goes."

Neo doesn't do anything.

Morpheus is like, "Remember – all I'm offering is the truth. Nothing more."

Spoiler alert/ADD Side Note: I went back and forth about using this whole Matrix reference because I was like, *"Maybe they haven't seen the Matrix."* And if you haven't seen it then you won't know exactly what I'm talking about. Also, I'm going to ruin a really big scene for you at a pivotal part of the movie. But then I was like, *"Wait if you haven't seen the Matrix then you have bigger problems in your life, starting with the fact that you're probably a douchebag."*

He chooses the red pill because he has to know.

Obviously.

Everyone always does. It seems to be humanly impossible for any of us to resist the truth. We just have to know, whatever the cost or the pain or the disappointment. It's like a drug. Dumb and reckless, we can't help ourselves.

That's why I always tell my new hires the same first thing. "Seriously. It's okay to take the blue bill." But every time they want the damn red pill. I mean, it's kind of a joke because I don't obviously have these magical red and blue pills on me, but they get the metaphor (they were all paying attention to the world and took the time to see an epic movie). They get that I'm telling them that they'll probably be happier if they don't learn what I know and wake up happily ignorant in their beds believing whatever they want. But they can't help themselves. They are hungry for power and knowledge within the world of the Internet where everyone else is just a user. They believed Gates when he said, "The day is quickly coming when every knee will bow down to a silicon fist, and you will all beg your binary gods for mercy." They want to understand the mysterious programming languages. They want the maps and keys and the cracks for the systems and they think it will all be revealed like codes streaming down in green right before their open eyes. And there we will be, all together, dressed in designer leather, running through the rain to save the rest of the world, like fucking superheroes.

I'm not the only one who fantasizes about the superhero world, I have learned.

I don't like leather much, though. It chafes. And I am currently not a superhero. (But then again, isn't that just EXACTLY what a superhero would say?) Also, I didn't invent the Internet. (That was Al Gore, LOL.) I never built a full operating system. (That was Bill Gates. ;)) I haven't developed an original programming language. So as far as I see it, I don't have any ownership in any of these things I've learned dicking around on the computer for hours on end. I have no problem showing everyone everything I know and bragging about it to everyone who will listen. That's just what I do. I can't help myself.

Side Note: Again, the editors tell me this is a book and not a blog. They want me to take out the LOL and the ;). But I was like, *"This is my book, suits. They stay in."* BTW, after I showed them my pre-sales numbers and how I'm going to sell about a gazillion copies of this book they were like, *"Okay. You know what you're doing."* This is me. Book. Blog. ADD. Side Notes. Cursing. Whatever. :P

So I was saying that I always give all my best shit away for free. (You can't imagine how many people have told me that I shouldn't do THAT, too!) The thing is, though, that all people really want—beyond any knowledge about web traffic and purchase patterns and sales psychology and algorithms—is a magic pill for making boat loads of money. That's the mistake they make. They think the red pill is a magic pill. It's not. All I can offer is the truth and nothing more. All I can tell you is what I do and how it works. All I can tell you is that you have to be willing to do what others are willing not to do.

We've been over this already, but I'll say it again. There is no magic pill, whatever color. There's no painless or miraculous fix for losing weight, for falling in love, for making money and living happily ever after. You make money by doing things that you are good at, that you stay with, that keep you interested, that capture your imagination, and that sometimes push the boundaries legally, ethically and morally.

I like money. I like making boat loads of it. But I also like to like what I'm doing and I like to work hard and put my everything into whatever it is that I am doing. Ultimately, I have become the best Internet Marketer walking this planet. Yes that sounds cocky, but it is also fact. We haven't exactly gotten there yet though, and I want you to understand that even in this lightning pace world we live in where nothing is sacred anymore and techie billionaires seem to be created overnight, being successful, being accomplished, and becoming wealthy takes time and work. In other words, I didn't always have my big house and my Ducati and an open invitation to party at the Playboy mansion.

We're still at the point when I was a geeked-out recluse living in a cave, remember?

By my second year at Western, I rarely ever came out in the daylight. All I cared about was gaming and writing programs. I was even writing hacks and cracks. I was a true hacker. I took existing code and hacked away until I broke through. This didn't make me a bad guy, BTW. That's just prejudice. You hear "hacker" and you immediately think "criminal." But that's not true. Somewhere along the way hackers got a bad rap, probably because of a few assholes that were doing things like hacking into websites for political purposes or into banks to steal money. Those guys ARE criminals. But that doesn't mean every hacker is a criminal. But if you still think—in your non h4x0r related view—that hacker=criminal, well then I guess I'm not a legitimate hacker because I never hacked into anything to do something illegal.

Side Note for Non-Techies: A hack is like a quick, "I hacked away at the config. file for this application until I found the one line of code that triggered registration and removed it." A software crack is an application that circumvents software security you are trying to get around. It's like, "I wrote a crack that fools this software into thinking I already paid for it." Hacks are quick and dirty. They're also permanent. Cracks take longer to write and usually need to be launched as their own application prior to the software.

I WAS a hacker. :P I got really good at understanding how viruses worked and the nature of cryptology. Viruses truly fascinated me. With a virus I could get into anyone's computer. I just had to get someone to download a program and then I'd be in. It works just like a Trojan horse. I never created a new virus. I didn't have to. There were already enough out there; it didn't make sense for me to spend my time inventing totally new ones. What I would do, instead, was renovate them. I would hack away at code from existing viruses until they did exactly what I wanted them to do. That was the easy part. The hard part was coming up with a way that would actually get people to download and install my renovated viruses. I came up with tons of unique ways. Without spiraling into a manual on hack tactics here, let me just say that the single best way to disguise Trojan horse type files is within a set of nudies. Guys are pretty simple. I know because I am a guy. I can tell you that if your audience is a bunch of horny guys who are looking to get off, well, you will always have an audience. We will do anything to get off, pretty much. You can hide pretty much anything behind nude photos and—I promise you—some guy will open it.

I'm not trying to teach you how to become a hacker or a programmer, here. I'm trying to entertain you a little bit. But I also want you to understand how I was discovering my talents. I think a lot of times we all feel pressure to bend ourselves into something we think we *should* be. But that will never make you happy. You have to be doing what you are naturally good at. Do that and do it a lot. Do what you are good at until you are the best [insert skill] walking the face of the Earth. (I guess that was another Side Note, ADD or otherwise.)

Hacking code and learning programing languages came really naturally to me. It's all a matter of working with algorithms, which are basically puzzles. For example, a serial number for Photoshop is based on an algorithm. When the software company distributes legitimate serial numbers they don't have some monkey manually writing unique numbers for everyone who purchases their software. That would be retarded. Instead, each number is computer-generated and that is all based on an algorithm. If you can decrypt that algorithm, by understanding patterns (that's a really simple way of putting it), then you can create an application that would randomly generate working serial numbers for that program. The other route is to look at the application and reverse engineer it. You look at the point when the registration number is verified and then circumvent that process. It was just a matter of following the code and the process. This stuff never got old for me. I would work on it for hours. As a bonus challenge, program companies were constantly trying to stay a step ahead of us hackers, putting up new walls to try and protect the spots where the magic happened. This only made the whole thing more fun.

Hopefully this doesn't trigger an investigation where a couple of official-looking dudes come knocking at my door with a warrant to search for a bunch of pirated software. Let me just be clear. I'm not in that business anymore. These days I buy all the software that we use. I never have a problem paying for a program that will help me make money. But back in the cave days, I couldn't afford 1500 bucks for something I needed. Not that it makes it any better or worse, I guess. At any rate, it was the reason.

Today it wouldn't be worth it for me to use pirated anything because there's a price to pay for that. First, it's illegal, although I suppose that wouldn't exactly deter me. Secondly, I am now too busy to spend time figuring out how to crack a program. Mostly, though, it's not reliable. That's the big problem. Using a crack instead of a legitimate program is like buying spare parts to build your own car. Chances are that a car like that is going to break down from time to time. When you're a grown up with two kids and your own businesses you can't have a car break down when you're going to the minimart for a quart of milk. It's the same thing with pirated software. If you can afford to live without the annoyance of a car that breaks down a lot and a version of Photoshop that doesn't work perfectly, you would. So I do.

But back in the day I couldn't afford what I needed and so I creatively found ways to get it anyhow. And in doing so I got really good at hacking and cryptology. It's like a doctor knowing anatomy. You can read all about it in the books, but you don't know shit until you take a gross anatomy class and start to get your hands into dead bodies. If you work in computers and really any sort of technology now, you have to know all the backend stuff. The only way you get with the guts is to get your hands dirty.   In all those hours by myself in my cave I was learning everything I could never learn in class or from a book. And it was fun.

Right around this time, I co-founded the very first chat channel to share Macintosh files. We called it #Macfilez and I was the The_Shark. Everything on there was pirated and accessible to the public. Under my alias I wrote a ton of the hacks and cracks and then we distributed the software on the chat channel. (BTW, AOL dorks refer to "chat channels" as "rooms.") As a bonus to the full versions of the software, we also included the cracks and hacks to make them work. And we offered all of it FOR FREE. Under the alias of The_Shark I became notorious and really well-respected within the hacker community.

I was invited to join a bunch of private hacker communities and conferences. DefCon was the biggest of them all and probably the most interesting. It's always held in Vegas and eventually it always gets shut down by the host hotel. All hands are on deck at the start because you have the greatest hackers in the world all under one roof. Regardless, every year they hack into the hotel's system—and these are no-joke CASINOS we're talking about—because that's what they do. They also have this thing called the Wall of Sheep, which is a projection on this massive wall of usernames and passwords from all the thousands of people who are using wireless around the premises to log into a website. It's their very visible way of being like, "We're in control and everyone else is a dipshit."

Anyhow, going to a panel discussion at DefCon is nuts. On one panel you have the guy who just got out of prison for hacking NASA sitting next to an FBI Internet Task Force Agent. The ironic part is that they are really good friends. Hell, they even educated each other by doing hacks and cracks together when they were younger. The only difference between them is which side of the game they're on. One guy hacks for fun and the other guy creates the security walls that are supposed to keep the criminals from breaching their networks and software. It's a matter of offense and defense. They both know the guts of the Internet, which has taken over the world as we knew it, and because of that they're all frickin' powerful. Those guys—the criminals and the government dudes—they're all cowboys. They know the truth and would never have taken anything but the red pill.

Gates wasn't far-off with his line, actually. The world does bow to the binary gods who can steal their passwords and shut down their Facebooks. Last year DefCon ended when those guys dumped cement powder into the hotel toilets for fun. You can imagine how that ended up. Pirates and cowboys and criminals all together—that's my kind of crew and the crew who knows exactly what you're doing online, right now. (Maybe think twice about clicking on that nude, okay? Just a word of friendly advice.)

As for my crew at Western, well they all graduated and moved out of our animal house. I didn't need a degree or anymore classes. I was a pirate and a cowboy already. I had been to Wonderland. I took the red pill and I know that the rabbit hole goes on and on and on.

11

Ever Questing

There is no unique picture of reality

-STEPHEN HAWKING

I don't know much about you. I don't know where you came from and what kind of crazy things you've experienced, which have shaped you into the person you are today. I haven't read your book, yet, okay? But even though I don't know you, I bet I know one thing about you.

You just wish you could be happier.

I'm right. I know it. You're searching.

Maybe you're looking for something cool to do this weekend so that you can brag about it later on Facebook, even if it actually sucked. Or maybe you're looking for that pair of jeans that will make your ass look not so fat. If you find that pair of jeans and you're at the cool spot, then maybe you'll find your soul-mate. Once all those things happen, everything will be perfect and you'll even get the job that you want, which of course will make you lots of money. You haven't found it all yet. I know. Because you still wish that you could just be happier.

Or maybe you've already found the right god and you're all set because He or She is going to take care of everything. (See I'm not a pig who thinks that a woman couldn't be God. Trust me. I think all women are goddesses to begin with.)

Good luck with all that hope and God stuff. I think it was Billy Bob Thornton in Bad Santa who said, "Hold out both hands. Hope in one, shit in another and see which one fills up faster."

That's my point and before I tell you more about my addiction to video games like EverQuest, I have a few things I need to put out there, starting with a rant about religion. It's a topic that fascinates me so much, I can't help myself.

Just about every person you meet is never completely happy. They are always looking for more and for that reason, they are the perfect consumers. The more you want, the more you can be manipulated. Or in other words, the more pain you're in, the more desperate you are for someone to come along and be like, "Hey, my friend, I was once like you and felt depressed. Then I started thinking, what if there was a product made by a guy just like us that figured out the "key" to finding dates online and getting laid. That's when I discovered the *Vagina Machine DVD Set*. And I gotta' tell you, it's CRAZY! Dude, it works like magic. Just look what all these people are saying about the *Vagina Machine DVD Set*..." And you're sitting there listening to the message and thinking it's brilliant and the DVDs are the very thing you've always needed, just like all those other douchebags on the infomercial. So you buy it.

I'm a marketer. Trust me. I'm lying to you.

I know what I'm talking about here. I have made millions of dollars selling people stuff on the Internet. I have a model for how it works and what I always show you. I call it the 3Ps and the formula is copyright pending (which doesn't really matter since I give all my best shit away for free). So here you go.

- **Pain.** You have a huge problem right now. (At least one!!)
- **Potential.** You are dying to know that there's a way to solve this problem.
- **Proof.** You're in luck! There IS a solution, JUST LOOK HOW IT WORKED FOR JIMMY!

If you understand even that tiny bit you will be successful in sales. And if you acknowledge that reality, perhaps you won't be such a dipshit consumer in the future. Maybe, just maybe, you'll even take a look at the religion that you follow because the guys in charge (and I mean that literally, because it's always the guys and never the ladies) certainly get my theory.

Every religion fits in perfectly to the 3P model.

- **Pain.** You have a huge problem right now: You are going to die at any time and then maybe go to a bad place where you could burn for eternity while being eaten, one toenail at a time, by millions of spiders. Forever and ever and ever. Yes, this is a huge problem.
- **Potential.** You are dying (before you actually do die) to know that there's a way to solve this problem. Instead of burning for eternity in a very bad place what if you could live forever and ever in a magical place with all of your friends and get laid everyday by a different beautiful virgin!?!?!?
- **Proof.** You're in luck! There is a solution and just look how it worked for Jimmy (or Abraham or Matthew or Ali al-Akbar)! All of the proof that you need is written in this really old book that is sacred and so you can't question it at all. But you don't need to be skeptical because the entire process for salvation is right here at your fingertips and IT'S GUARANTEED TO

HAPPEN TO YOU (as long as you do what we say). We are pulling back the curtains and giving you the secrets to eternal life and happiness. YAY!

That's exactly how every fucking thing is sold and how it's been sold forever. This is how humans tick. Everyone is looking for the product that is going to be the real magic bullet. The whole world is still searching.

ADD Side Note: Earlier I said, "Trust me. I am lying." That is because all marketers are liars. We make up the magic stories about the products we are slinging. Did you know that 8 companies tried to sell the crockpot and failed until 1 company told the "right" magic story about what the crockpot will do for consumers? **PAY ATTENTION FUCKERS!** NOBODY buys a product for what it actually does. They buy it because they were sold on the story of what the product was going to do for them. How many kitchen appliances have you purchased? Do you have a crockpot and a juicer and a mixer and the thing they actually, literally call the Magic Bullet™? Well then, some smart marketer sold you too. But the truth is all that crap is just collecting dust in a cabinet somewhere behind the new crap that you just bought. None of it will see the light of day, probably for years.

Okay. Back to the story.

Everyone graduated from Western and I moved back to Moline.

Again, I lived at my mom's crib, but only for a few weeks this time around. I wanted to move out. You know, it's hard to rub one out when your mom's around all the time. Anyway, that was my motivation for getting off my ass and finding a job. Pretty easily I found another computer gig to pass the time. The shop was another ISP called Internet Revealed and I was hired to work customer support from 3pm – 11 pm at ten bucks an hour. All of this was fine. What made it awesome was that my boss was THE SHIT.

He was really laid back and nice but most importantly, he was totally into video games. This meant that he not only didn't care if we spent our time between calls dicking around, gaming online—he actually encouraged it. At the time this was nearly as good as getting laid each day by a different, beautiful virgin because this was right when the game EverQuest came out.

This game was epic and I mean, EPIC. Imagine playing Dungeons and Dragons in 3D with 100,000 other people while on steroids, with an 8-ball and six shots of 8-Hour Energy™. That's about how exciting this game was. It's a role playing game that takes you to a fantasy world called Norrath where you are part of complicated and eternal quest in which good will overtake evil or evil will take over everything. It was medieval and futuristic and philosophical and gritty and challenging and fun and completely consuming. I poured myself into my quest to dominate that world. That's all I cared about.

EverQuest could be brutal though. You would play for DAYS and then one death would mean you lost hours (if not days) of hard work advancing your character. Everyone at the shop was totally into the game and pretty advanced. My boss' wife was a real bitch from hell and the only time he could play games was at work. But this worked out for him because he had the entire tech team play with him so we could "twink" him out with badass equipment, and help him "level" his character without any risk of dying. It was pretty awesome. Everyone was happy.

All together there were six of us at Internet Revealed. The job was really basic. I just fielded customer support calls. It wasn't exactly taxing. On top of that, we were all major wise-asses who loved screwing around. When the phone rang, one of us would answer it and someone would be whining about how their server wasn't loading and we'd be like, "Hmmmmm. Yea…..Mmmmhmmmm….Yea. Now, did you reboot it? Well, you need to reboot it. Okay, reboot it now and I'll put you on hold." We'd get back on the line in five minutes and the jackass would say it still wasn't working and we'd be all, "I see. Okay. Well that means you have to reboot it again. You have to reboot it three times. I'll put you on hold again and be right back." The thing was that rebooting didn't really do a whole lot. Mostly, we were just screwing around. The best thing about this whole set-up was that it was super easy to be playing EverQuest the whole time, while we were "working."

Because my day didn't start until 3pm, I was only with those guys for a few hours. Everyone went home at 5pm, except me and another other guy by the name of Tony Petrizi. We sat around together, screwing with the client calls and playing EverQuest until he left at 8. And then it was just me and my character for three hours in the dark. The most exciting thing that ever happened at the office at night was if my character died and then I happened to yell something like, "FUCK!" into the phone while some dipshit was rebooting. Then I'd have to apologize and be like, "Okay, so have you rebooted? You need to reboot. I'm going to put you on hold."

That was what most days were like.

It doesn't actually sound exciting, from the outside. That's because you weren't in my Norrath world. I had everything I wanted there. It was a whole life. Even though I was an individual player, in order to progress through the levels you have to build a "guild," or a community with the other people who are playing. I virtually hooked up with this beautiful young wood-elf named Sweetnipples19. She had such a nice ass. She would send me private messages, flirting with me and telling me how horny she was or whatever. We had awesome sex where she would bend her character over and I would move my guy behind her like a porn star. The whole time we'd be messaging each other back and forth and she'd be like "It feels so good. You're my druid stud." And then sometimes we'd just cuddle.

We spent every day together like that, for months, until I asked her to marry me. We had a really decked-out wedding. All of my friends stood next to me as we exchanged vows. One of my friends went a little nuts and brought a ton of alcohol. The entire wedding party got wasted. I could barely control my character. Sadly, the party was crashed by an evil gang of trolls and necromancers from an unfriendly faction. In our drunken state, we didn't stand a chance. The wedding ended in a slaughter. We all died.

In a new life, Sweetnipples19 and I made a home. We adopted other players as our kids. We did all the things I never thought I'd do in my real life. I didn't have a real girlfriend. I never was the guy who got the girl. I sure as shit never thought I'd get married. Remember, I wasn't even expecting to live much past 30. In Norrath, besides the trolls and necromancers who were lurking about, things were pretty dope. I had everything. I was awesome and I totally loved it. I guess you can say that I was addicted because, beyond getting up and going to work and telling people to reboot their DSL connections, it's all I ever did.

Unfortunately, I have to tell you that Sweetnipples19 turned out to be a guy named Roy. I felt a bit sick to my stomach the day I found out, kind of like the guy in *The Crying Game*. But overall, despite my divorce with Roy, things were still pretty sweet in Norrath. In the virtual settlement I ended up with both our Platinum Bands and the Cloak of Flames. I also got custody of our horse on alternating weekends. So, all in all, I would say our romance ended amicably. Oh, and I eventually traded the Platinum Wedding Bands for a FBSS. That stands for Flowing Black Silk Slash, which was a pretty big deal if you didn't know.

You build currency in the world of Norrath by mastering skills like hunting and swimming, but also basket-weaving and metallurgy and pottery. Within the game your avatar actually has to complete drills that teach you these skills. In order to be really good, you have to spend a ton of time playing. In fact, after a while, it wasn't like playing as much as it was practicing. It got so bad that I didn't even go to Thanksgiving or Christmas for two years. I couldn't justify spending that much time away from what was really important and pressing.

And it wasn't just me.

They did a study a while back that said if Norrath was a real country it would be the sixth leading exporter of goods and services. In 2002, a dude named Edward Castronova reported that Norrath would be the 77th richest country in the world, taking a place between Russia and Bulgaria with a GDP per capita that was higher than both China and India. So I guess you could say that we were an efficient and productive bunch of chars. (Char—that's more in-game lingo. It means character, if you couldn't guess.)

Eventually I logged one year and six months of active in-game playtime.

I guess, "addicted" might have been an understatement.

The only thing I loved more than being in that world was dominating within that world. I realized about halfway into my addiction that there had to be a way to bound ahead of all the other chars—a way I could level myself ahead even faster than I had already done. I was sitting all alone at my customer support post late one night when I realized the angle. I had to find a way to cut out sleep.

At this point I was playing from the time I awoke, through work, and then back in my empty one-bedroom apartment until I passed out. But that wasn't enough. I decided that if my avatar spent all the hours while my physical self was sleeping doing the mundane work of skill building (fifteen swim drills or twenty weaving exercises) I could devote my waking play time to the activities like killing or exploring, which actually required my attention. So I wrote programs for my character to do exactly that while I slept every night. Before long I was the first druid to reach Level 50.

It worked perfectly.

For a while.

The only problem was that I was now alone. I had cheated myself so far ahead that the battles I had to fight against wizards and dragons and warlords were impossible without help. My character died a number of deaths, the penalty for which is ridiculously fucking harsh. Obviously you get knocked back in terms of level experience but you are also in danger of losing all of the stuff you have gathered and the skills you have acquired. Your corpse and gear remain wherever you fell, but as a player you return to your "bind" point naked. If you can't make it back to the zone to recover your corpse where you left it, you are resurrected without everything you earned and you're screwed like a pooch. And then you mourn—like seriously mourn and fall into depression—real-world, waking life, medication-necessary depression.

I'm not exaggerating one bit.

People have actually committed suicide because of this game. I'm pretty sure Tipper Gore is against it because the statistics are staggering. Go look it up, if you care. I can tell you that at the peak of its popularity there were a half a million player/addicts. It's been called NeverRest and EverCrack. One of the most publicized tragedies to come out of Norrath was the suicide of Shawn Wooley. I won't go into his entire story except to say his mother eventually founded Online

Gamers Anonymous. I'm not making this shit up. It's as serious as any other addiction out there. Anytime you care about getting so much of one thing that nothing else matters anymore—that's a problem.

I was totally addicted, but I couldn't get any farther. I just kept dying and falling more and more behind because of the harsh penalties. I became seriously depressed because I couldn't handle the failure.

So I quit.

Well, it wasn't exactly that abrupt.

Side Note: Koreans frickin' love EverQuest. I don't know why, exactly, but it's definitely a thing with them.

I decided to sell my character and a Korean bought it from me on eBay for $1400. You see, if you have a lot of money you don't have to devote your life to getting to an exciting Norrath level. You can just buy one. And then you'll be happy.

Happily ever after for the Korean. Happily ever after for me.

I was hoping.

But my compulsion didn't go away and my depression didn't let up.

I had to admit that I wasn't done with this thing. I had to find a way back in—a better way to play. I wanted a more universal existence within Norrath—something that would be more powerful and more fulfilling and not held to the rules of the game. There are these entities called GMs which are Sony's in-game representatives. If you are skilled enough you can apply to become a GM and receive a free account as a non-player character. You make a few bucks on the side for settling minor in-game disputes between characters but most importantly you are invulnerable and immortal. You're kind of like a quasi-god. You can do almost anything including granting full resurrections, summoning any item, or summoning a player to any zone within the game.

When you're a GM the deal is that you only exercise your divine powers to address issues like a bug or to reimburse a lost item or penalize a retard who isn't playing "nice." I didn't exactly see it that way, though. When I finally became a GM, I was fixated on the fact that I was invulnerable. I had the power to kill any other non-player character, like the most badass dragons. There was real value in that power. I knew there was an angle there.

One of the main components of competition within EverQuest is collecting items. You can only get the most valuable items at the end of a major battle. For example, there are these things called Planes—i.e. the Plane of Fear, the Plane of Hate—which require characters to amass an army and coordinate an attack. It takes about eighty VERY highly skilled players to get through a plane and it's at least a ten hour commitment. Once I spent a full twenty-four hours on a plan run. But there was a huge reward for getting through the Plane. The last "bosses" always looted some amazing items. The items would be "rolled on," which meant that you were rolling against the other seventy-nine players for a shot at getting the item. They were always really cool things, but sometimes you'd even get a really rare drop— something like a flaming sword. Anyhow, your odds of actually getting the one thing at the end weren't good.

I never liked those odds.

As a GM I was special. I could defeat any enemy alone. That was obviously good. But in-game, a GM gets no reward for a defeat or value from their magical cross-bow. I didn't have a running score. I wasn't a real player. Also, as a GM there is a log kept on everything you do. Killing everything wasn't a big deal because that was something I was responsible for doing whenever a Plane needed to be re-set. That's exactly why I had the power in the first place and wouldn't be suspicious. But if it was reported that I was on level 43 looting a monster by myself, that would be a major red flag on my log.

I needed a friend to help.

One of my friends, Saldo Silvermoon, was really established within level 50 and I told him my plan. I knew I could trust him because we had a history. Back when I was a druid, we used to hunt together. Also, he was the best man at my wedding to Sweetnipples19. Anyhow, Saldo was a good guy and as soon as I told him my plan, he loved it. It was really very simple. Since I was invulnerable I would go through the top level and whack all the monsters and then I would use my divine powers to summon Saldo to that zone. All Saldo had to do was loot the item from the boss. No more one in eighty. The whole process took about fifteen minutes. We did this every day for eight hours and he would end up with a huge bag full of the very rare items.

Right now you're probably like, *"So what?! Who cares about magical crossbows and flaming swords? There's no street value in that virtual crap!"*

WRONG!

Remember the Korean? Well, characters weren't the only things for sale on eBay. You could buy anything you wanted or needed in-game from someone on eBay. Basically, I became a supplier for highly-prized in-game EverQuest items. We had huge demand. Depending on the rarity of the item, I would sell stuff anywhere between $10 and $1000. My weekly revenue was about $10K. The whole thing was profit minus the 20% cut I gave Saldor through PayPal.

Now you're probably like, "Well, *why the fuck would anyone pay $1000 for an imaginary sword?!?!?"*

The answer is—TIME. It could take someone 20,000 hours of playing time to find a specific sword. If you ask yourself how much 20,000 hours of your time is worth, it starts to make a lot more sense.

The whole thing was brilliant. We made thousands of dollars a week for chilling in-game.

Suddenly, I wasn't so depressed. The money was awesome, but that wasn't what curbed the depression. It felt good to be doing something new. I felt like I was running and gunning—doing something no one else had thought of yet. That's when I'm really in my element and when I'm having fun. And when I'm having fun, I dominate.

But of course I got a little too full of myself and said something to someone that I shouldn't have. I had also completely neglected my functions as a GM and hadn't responded to any in-game petitions for weeks. Sony deactivated my account and that was that—a total fucking bummer. I probably should have saved some of the cash, in hindsight.

Meanwhile, back at Internet Revealed the happy situation was about to become very unhappy thanks to the boss' bitch wife. (You have to see where this is going.)

Apparently, Internet Revealed was doing okay but the bitch wife decided it was time to quit her job, come work with us and supervise productivity. She observed our habits for one day and realized that they weren't exactly getting the best return from our little tech support team. She called a meeting to announce that during work hours our gaming habits were going to cease, effective immediately. In the future, any extra time we might have between customer support calls would be used to stuff the billing statements for mailing.

It didn't take superhero skills to predict this turn of events. The guys and I knew she would come down with something similar. In a hushed meeting beforehand we all agreed to unite in protest against the bitch wife, if necessary. So after she laid down the new law I was all pumped. I stood up and was like, "This is bullshit! We are making peanuts! We're not going to stuff envelopes!" I was practically yelling like a fists-in-the-air revolutionary or something. I expected to turn around to see my boys standing up behind me shouting, "Screw this! Screw this! Screw this!" But nobody made a damn peep.

Needless to say, they fired me the next day.

Again, I had nothing in the world but my balls and a crappy one bedroom apartment. That's where I spent the next eight months. That period of time is like a total blank in my memory. Nothing happened. I couldn't find a job. Not a single, dumb job. Not even a job at a gas station. So I sat on my ass and played games online. I can't even remember what the games were. It was kind of like I just turned off.

I still had to pay my rent and bills though. You can't magically turn that stuff off. And I still needed to eat. I used three credit cards for everything. I got cash advances—as much as I could, as often as I could. I didn't know when that would turn off, too, so I just took as much as possible. By the time I maxed out all three cards, I was thirty grand in debt.

That didn't scare me. When you're really low down and depressed, you don't care about much. When you don't care about much you also don't scare easily. I was particularly not scared about the debt because I had no intention of paying it back. Remember, I honestly didn't expect to be alive six or seven years down the road and a dead man doesn't worry about his debt. I wasn't concerned even though I had no plan. In all the crazy shit I have been through, this was by far, the lowest point. I honestly didn't care about a single thing.

Have you ever been truly without hope? Like I said earlier, I don't know you. I don't know if you have or if you can even imagine it. It's not a desperate place. It's not a suicidal place. It's worse. It's just a place where you sit with literally no life, no reason to move and no desire to make it otherwise.

Oh, and one more thing…

I was still a virgin.

12
Wells Fargo Redemption

Get busy living or get busy dying.

-ANDY DUFRESNE,

The Shawshank Redemption

Jesus. This has gotten really depressing.

But, trust me. Everything turns out really good in the end. You have to just keep reading. Go grab a cocktail or something if you need a little refreshment. I get it. I know that last phase was a total bummer. It even seems worse now, as I'm remembering it. I'm prone to depression and anxiety, naturally, so shitty circumstances don't exactly motivate me to go looking for rainbows. But I've also told you that my brain never stops and even when the odds are totally against me and it looks like I have a loser's hand, I get off looking for the angle I need to win, or cheat—however you want to look at it.

A lot of crazy shit had happened to me—a lot of which, I sort of created. The thing about me is that I'm a crafty dude and I know that I'm always going to find a way to get through all the shit and win. That's the great thing about me, maybe the greatest. But having good friends can also come in handy.

Spoiler Alert: This is where things really start to get good.

Moline was almost as depressed as I was. The entire Quad City area was a real shithole because most of the manufacturing plants had shut down. That led to a massive unemployment problem and whole neighborhoods in foreclosure. Or let me put it this way, no one was buying pimped out stereo systems at Best Buy. There were no jobs and no money.

Like I was telling you before, I sat in my crap apartment for eight months. It might have been longer. The whole time is really fuzzy. All I know is that I played a lot of video games and was really depressed and really in debt. But I didn't completely close myself off from my friends. They've always been important to me so I keep the lines going.

At this point, with no prospects, my friend, Eric Tagtmeier gets to play a little hero role in the story. He was working at the First Savings Bank in Moline and when the Regional Systems Administrator job opened, he got me in the door. So FINALLY—after months of sitting on my ass playing video games in the dark like I was a fourteen year old, I had a lead. I figured that Moline did not have a huge batch of techie talent to compete for this type of position, so even though I had no experience with bank or financial systems, I figured I had a good shot.

I was right. The bank contacted me almost immediately. Based on their eagerness I was totally confident in my chances. I figured all I had to do was show up for the interview, exuding confidence, and everything would work out. The thing that all tech geeks know is that we know a whole lot more than everyone else. You just whip out the lingo and you're elevated into a super realm that any mid-level HR person can't understand. And you're in. It's true.

But you have to show up to the interview. That's crucial.

If you stayed up all night long playing video games and slept through your alarm, missing your scheduled interview, then you have pretty much fucked yourself good. Unless there is the small chance that—between the circumstances and the weather conditions and the quality of your imagination and the size of your balls—you can cook up an excuse that the manager might buy for a second. Like (*and this is, of course, just an example*), let's say I did sleep through my interview for the only job prospect I had in eight months. Then I would call the manager and—with a convincing amount of panic in my voice—tell him that I had just been in a car accident. I would say that I had been on my way to the interview in the rain when the car in front of me slammed on his breaks and then I rammed into the back of his Beemer. I would apologize—really sincerely—and hope that, *as I had just returned from the hospital,* there was some way we could reschedule for the following day.

Side Note: To tell a story well you really have to go all-in. Sometimes that means using props and shit. Like, if you are trying to sell the fact that you were in a car accident recently, maybe you show up with a neck brace or something. You can't overthink it—you just have to go balls out. If you can't get a neck brace, well then you better get a damn good limp going. Do something to really sell it, something that might even convince yourself that the story is 100% true. It's like George Constanza said, "It's not a lie if YOU believe it."

Anyhow, the next day I limped into my interview with the bank manager. And wouldn't you know it, we hit it off right away and he made me the new Regional Systems Administrator for the First Savings Bank of Moline. The "accident" was never an issue.

This was Enron time, which basically sucked for everyone who lost jobs and retirement funds and everything. But selfishly, it was a perfect time to come into the banking industry. The WorldCom swindle happened right after and then the government started cranking out all sorts of legislation and banking regulations, like Sarbanes-Oxley. A few years before that, they introduced the Gramm-Leach-Bliley Act (GLB).

Without getting balls deep into legislation here, all you need to know is that these laws had to do with the way information was handled and protected. They introduced a whole new set of policies in terms of data security, integration, collection and disclosure.

The girl who had the job before me was an idiot. She didn't know her ear from her vag. On top of that, she was a bitch. Actually, saying she was a bitch wouldn't do her justice. This chick was a banshee. So this idiot banshee—who had absolutely no authority or credentials in system or network administration—had implemented a shit-ton of systems and policies that were a complete waste of time. She did such a "good job" with all of that, she got a promotion and I came in to take over all the things related to information security and regulation. It's true that I didn't have any actual credentials in system or network administration. It wasn't like I could frame my invitations from DefCon or put my hacks and cracks on my resume as bullet points. But I knew what I was doing, which is more than I can say for anyone else they could have possibly hired at the time.

That was enough to get me in the door, but to stay white collar, I had to start collecting legitimate credentials. The bank sent me to an endless number of certification courses and seminars until I was the most decorated systems dude in the Quad Cities. They invested a lot of time and money in me. Now, you would think—because they spent all that time and money to get me certified—that would only make me more valuable. It's like when a guy is trying to pick up a chick at a bar. If right away a girl is like, "Let's go do it," you might hold off a while, suspicious that this girl is psycho or convinced that you could do better. But if you spend all night long pumping drinks into the same chick and whipping out all kinds of interesting conversation, then you have made a significant investment and you're not letting that girl go home with some other jack-off. I thought it was the same thing. I thought I was the girl getting all the free drinks. I didn't think they were going to let me go.

Okay, it wasn't *exactly* that simple.

After a few weeks, I got bored. The skills and credentials I had acquired were far beyond what I needed to administer First Saving's systems. It was a small bank. We didn't have a lot of customers, which meant I wasn't dealing with a lot of information or money. Of course I did some encryption work to keep everything protected, but honestly, no one was trying to hack into this bank.

I spent most of my time each week running these mind-numbing staff trainings. It was like the same thing over and over again. I would be like, "Who remembers the three classifications levels for our files?" And they'd look at me like I was speaking another language. And I'd have to be all nice like, "Okay. It's pretty simple people. We have 'shared,' 'private' or 'classified.' Let's review again." Bang. Shoot my brains out. Boring. I lost the little patience I had for those idiots and became a lot less visible. I also started gaming during the day, just to keep my brain working and to stay sane. It was more fun to sit at my desk and screw around online than deal with these idiots.

So fine—you could say that I was hiding at my desk, but I wasn't neglecting my responsibilities. I did what I always do. I found a better way to get something done. I put my job on automatic and I had the entire system running perfectly. Playing video games at my desk didn't change any of that. Everything probably would have been fine, except—don't forget about Leslie, the banshee. Technically, I worked *under* her and let me tell you she was definitely one who got off on riding you. :P

Leslie had put policies in place that actually cost the bank a lot of money. For one thing, she made it mandatory for the bank to buy all our hardware from one supplier (who just happened to be her friend). That guy had a huge mark-up on his supply so I started going through other, much less expensive vendors. She did not like that and went running off to tell on me. That kind of shit happened all the time. When I stopped holding meetings and started sitting at my computer all day, well, then she had even better complaints to take to management. Now for whatever reason (he was fucking her), the manager loved her. He loved her (like I said, he was fucking her), she hated me (she was a totally insecure banshee), and eventually she pulled rank. You can figure out how that ended. I was sent packing.

But I do want to say here that I'm not the kind of guy to call people out. LOL. Who am I kidding? Yes, I totally am. That manager's name was Steve. Steve I hope you're reading this book so you know that I know that you were totally fucking Leslie. And I want everyone else to know that Leslie wasn't even hot and she had less than average tits.

Anyhow, I was out on my ass and I was still in a lot of credit card debt. I was happy to work. I mean, I wanted to work my way out of debt. (No one could possibly LIKE living under the abuse of collection calls. Talk about something that could drive a person bat shit paranoid). I had a crazy ton of qualifications to work. There just weren't any jobs left in Moline.

There's an old story that goes like this. A guy is walking down the street and he falls into a hole. It came out of nowhere—this incredibly deep hole—but once he's down at the bottom there's nothing the guy can do but wait for something to happen. He needs someone to help him. Eventually a doctor walks past and throws down a prescription. The guy holds it in his hand, but he can't even read it in the dark. It's no help. Then a priest walks past and yells a prayer down to the man, but he can't really hear it. Nothing happens and it's no help. Eventually the guy's friend walks past and he jumps right down into the same hole. The guy turns to his friend and is like, "Well that's no help. Now we're both down here." But the friend smiles and says, "Yeah but I've been down here before and I know the way out."

I actually don't know if it's an old story or not. It's definitely old in the sense that I heard it one night when I was up late, watching an old episode of *The West Wing*. Aaron Sorkin probably just made it up. It doesn't matter. The point is so true. There's nothing more helpful in a time of desperation than a friend who has been there before. The guy at the bottom of the hole needed his friend to jump in to get out. It's just like Andy Dufresne and Red needed each other's help in Shawshank Prison. Everybody needs friends. I have a long list. But for the purposes of this chapter I'm only mentioning two. First there was EricTagtmeier. Then there was George Schaeffer.

This is where George enters.

You're just meeting George now, but I have known George most of my life. He was the closest thing to a best friend that I can imagine. George was the senior security dude for Saks in Des Moines where he lived with his wife and his baby son in a modest two bedroom house. After I got fired from First National I was down in a deep hole without any foreseeable options. So I called up my friend, George. He told me to get the hell out of Moline and get my ass to Iowa. I was like, "Nah. I don't have any money." And he was like, "YES. You don't need money to start with. You're moving in with me."

But hang on a sec. There's one last Moline escapade that I just can't forget to tell you first.

Before I got fired from First Savings, while I was fucking around all day online, I discovered this great little thing known as Yahoo Dating. This was a brilliant discovery by me. I was a regular Casanova online. (Remember Sweetnipples19?) Online I could be confident and witty and forward and handsome. Basically I spent the entire last month at my bank job prowling and wooing the lovely ladies of Yahoo.

I started by emailing a few girls—the ones I figured weren't *too far* out of my league. And one of them was actually online at the time. She wasn't anything to write home about—totally just okay looking, but she was *there*. Beggars can't be choosers, ya' know? So, I sent her a picture of my fatass and she wasn't shocked or anything. There wasn't much to read between the lines with that chick. After a couple of IMs, I got the picture. Well—I got the literal pictures she sent me, obviously, but I also got the PICTURE because she actually said, "I'm 19. I'm horny. I want to come over and have sex with you." And I was thinking, "*This is totally one of my friends fucking with me. Oh wait…Oh shit…What if this is Roy!?!?*"

I figured the only way I could confirm who she was and if she was real was if she actually called me. So she did. And—Ring. Ring—there was this cute little voice saying all sorts of dirty stuff and asking if she could come over and have crazy sex with me. I was like, "Uhhh….yeaaaaa?!?" and scrambled to make my little crap apartment, somewhat presentable.

I was so frickin' nervous waiting for her. My heart was racing out of control because I knew she was going to knock on my door, take one look at me, and leave right away before having all the crazy sex with me like she promised. And then it happened. There was a knock on the door. *OH SHIT! THE MOMENT OF TRUTH.* She came in. She didn't head for the hills. She was built like a brick shithouse and she was also missing a few teeth but—whatever—I didn't care. She was a girl, just about 19, and most importantly, she wasn't Roy.

This chick knew how to be "very friendly." Now, by "very friendly," I mean that she basically raped me. Wait, let me clarify this so no one gets their panties in a bundle and I don't offend any girls who had that night when they didn't say "no" even though they didn't say "yes." In this "raping" I was a very willing participant. In fact, the only way any sex was happening that night was for her to basically rape me, because

I was so damn shy. I was a 25 year old virgin who only knew how to do it by myself, in my imagination or online.

God, I am so pissed that I can't remember her name. I should remember her name because I want to say thank you. She was the girl who could suck the chrome off of a trailer hitch (as my dad might say). We hooked up a bunch of times and it was always totally casual. I wish I could just remember her name because she played such a huge role in my life. So I'm just going to call her Suckface19.

> Dear Suckface19,
> If you are out there reading this, I just want to say thank you. You honestly played a huge role in my life. I know we only had those magical three minute sessions (sometimes five) together but I want you to know that I cherish them. Getting laid was a HUGE game changer for me. So, thank you. ;)
> -Jeremy

I'll say it again. Getting laid was a HUGE game changer for me.

I couldn't believe what I had been missing out on. And I couldn't believe how easy it was to get a girl into bed (or to drag me into bed) after years of thinking that no one would want me. So I emailed more girls and found out there were no shortage of Yahoo girls I could say "thank you" to.

Just before I left Moline I met this polyamorous chick. Right up front in our first IM conversation she told me that she was married but that in her relationship, she and her husband both took other lovers. I had no problem with that. It was exciting, even. I picked her up for our date a few nights later and we went to see *American Pie*. I didn't actually see most of the movie, though, because we made out like teenagers, slurping on each other's faces and everything.

I couldn't wait to get out of the theatre and back to my apartment. But she didn't want to go to my crib. She insisted we go to hers. My dick was so hard I could barely steer the damn car let alone think that her husband might walk in on us, so I agreed, like—whatever! This girl was HOT. She was way out of my league and so I would have done pretty much anything she wanted. I just really wasn't expecting what she had in mind.

We walked into her place and there was her husband, sitting in his La-Z-Boy watching *CSI: Miami*. And I was like, *"Oh fuck. Not good."* But she didn't flinch. She grabbed my hand and sat me down on the couch right by her side, RIGHT NEXT TO HER HUSBAND, and proceeded to mount me and start making out like, licking my face making out. I'm trying my best to lightly pry her paws off of me and at least politely peck her cheek while she's full-out mauling me. I mean her husband was RIGHT THERE (looking creepy as shit may I add). I whispered to her, "Why don't we go somewhere else?" And as she was sucking my ear she was like, "It's okay. He likes to watch."

HOLY FUCK! People actually do this.

That's all I could think as I excused myself to run to the bathroom where I called my mom. Yep. I called my mom. I made her promise to never to speak to me ever again of this phone call and to never ask me any questions about it. I just needed her to call me back in twenty seconds. Thank God for my mom in the clutch.

I walked back into the den and clapped my hands like I was ready to get it on with the chick in front of her creepy husband and then my phone rang. "Oh my God! You're KIDDING ME?! Oh NO!! OH NO!!!" I yelled into my phone, while rolling my eyes and shaking my head in my best act of disbelief. I hung up the phone and was like, "I'm so sorry (you sick freakoids), but I gotta' go."

And like that, I was out of there.

A week or so later I finally left Moline, ready to start pulling myself out of my hole along with George's help.

I have sat around trying to think of fitting ways to be able to thank George for all that he did for me and I just can't. There is no way to appropriately thank someone for basically saving your life. He was so warm and accommodating. This guy, with his family in his two bedroom apartment, pretty much demanded that I come and live with him, never minding the sacrifices they would have to make for me. They put a roof over my head and fed me in the beginning but what's more—HE GAVE ME HIS BED. I was too fat to fit on his couch so once I arrived in Des Moines, George moved onto his couch and his wife slept on the floor in their son's room. I didn't deserve that type of kindness but they gave it to me nonetheless.

Immediately I was completely astounded by how much more life there was in Des Moines compared to the depression of the Quad Cities. There were dozens of banks there that I could apply to and a handful of them actually actively recruited me because of the experience I had, but more importantly, because of the certifications I held. In the post 9/11 world, the certifications—the proof that you knew what you were doing with information security—was key. Corporations and financial institutions needed to have in-house personnel with the certifications I already had. I literally was a financial asset to the company that would hire me because they wouldn't have to pay for me to attain these certifications.

Remember the metaphor from before about a guy picking up a chick at a bar? Basically I was like the girl that hung out with another dude who spent a ton of time and money getting me wet. First Savings was the sucker that got me all attractive and now I had my pick of the litter. Or something like that.

I decided to take a job as the Lead Unix Security Manager for all of Wells Fargo Financial (WFF). My responsibilities included writing security policies for each department and their document classifications, conducting ongoing server audits, advising the virus, network and server teams on all security measures, leading all in-house security education and practices and generally monitoring and guarding the security of the entire institution. It was a blast. I loved it and for a solid chunk of time I was actually obsessed with my day job.

I was the WFF rock star. But I was also the dick because I played the role of Big Brother to everyone. I monitored what everyone did online and told people what they could and couldn't do. I blew the whistle on bad practices. Sometimes I even wore this fake badge around just to screw with people. It was fun. Everything was fun except catching the child pornographers. You wouldn't believe how many people have that scary shit on their computers at any given time in any given company. But when you're in my role, your responsibility is just to find the porn. I never had any knowledge about how it got there—technically. All I knew was that if it ever popped up I would see it. Then I had to confiscate the hard drive and then contact HR who would terminate the person immediately and permanently label them as a twisted fucker. I'm not saying I sympathize with child pornographers. They're severely fucked up and deserve everything that's coming to them. Just knowing that there are a good amount of them out there is disturbing enough. But it also affected me knowing that every once in a while an innocent person might be getting ruined forever. I couldn't do anything about it, though. I just wish I didn't know how often the whole thing happens.

Other than that stain on my daily life, I really loved my job. I went above and beyond, because you know, that's just me. When I'm into something, I'm all in.

I especially loved working with viruses. When any terminal in our system would get hit with a virus it was my ultimate responsibility to make sure that we could detect it instantly and then eradicate it. Actually, it was the virus team's primary responsibility to deal with all this shit, but it was my role to advise them; I made it my ultimate responsibility. The thing about viruses is that the people who distribute them are crafty. They can package them into anything you might download online. The end user (you) has no idea that when they install Yahoo Instant Messenger, for example, that they might be installing an extra hidden little virus at the same time. (It's called binding— pronounced with a short "I", just so you know and don't sound like a retard in conversation).

At home I had an isolated computer that I used to invent all sorts of shit. I binded existing viruses in all sorts of ways; I wrote my own viruses and I distributed them to different people at work through spoofs. For example, I would spoof someone's wife and send them a message with a heart that said, "Honey open this. I made it for you." He'd open it and then later that day in the middle of a busy office the program would take over his computer making his screen flash and sounding a blaring alarm. It sounds kind of mean, but—come on—it was research. I needed to know what kind of stuff people would fall for and how to detect it and kill it. And yes—it was also a lot of fun.

I completely revolutionized the IT department. Leading the virus team, we wrote dozens of programs to control viruses that were strangling other institutions. Also I wrote a password reset script, which was one single thing that made the entire company's life easier. You see, before my script, if someone had to reset her password, she would have to contact the Help Desk to clear the account and set up a temporary password. From an interface perspective it seems like a simple enough task. But the logistics involved on the backend were actually really complicated for the programmer to manually command. So one night I wrote a macro (like the macro I created to automate my character in

EverQuest). Before we installed it we ran a timed comparison. Manually the entire process took three minutes. With my macro it became instantaneous. That was a big deal.

For stuff like that I was named technology employee of the month from among a total of 1400 IT pawns. It felt good the first time and even better when I was named a second time. It was really gratifying to get that legitimate recognition for what I was doing and thinking about and obsessing over for once.

It's not reaching in the least to say that I revolutionized that company. The security policies that I wrote are still the policies they use today. If you went into a branch tomorrow and someone said to you, "Blah, blah, blah…it's a security thing." You could ask to see the written policy and when they'd whip it out of a drawer right there you'd see my name in black and white. I know because I've done it. All my companies are still with Wells Fargo because I trust their security policies, obviously. And I love to call bullshit when anyone tells me something completely ludicrous, which is justified by the blanket of "security policy." I love to make that guy pull out the manual and say, "I know you're full of shit because I know the policies. I wrote them. That's my name right there. See—Jeremy R. Schoemaker." That never, ever gets old.

What did get old was the lack of compensation I felt I was receiving. Sure, I got plenty of recognition. And it felt great. My chest was all puffed out with pride, but I was still getting the same measly 2% standard-of-living raise as the 9-5 monkey sitting in a cubicle across from me. I was revolutionizing the company, but all they could do was put my name on a plaque.

I stayed at Wells Fargo for a while longer and that time was really my redemption. It was the turning point from living like a man who expected to die to a man who was finally ready to live with rainbows and butterflies and orgasms that would one day explode into a family.

Which brings me to my wife.

13
Leaps of Faith

You only have to do a few things right in your life so long as you don't do too many things wrong.

-Warren Buffett

Don't be misled by my title. This isn't a religious, churchy thing. In fact this is the chapter where I'm going to tell you about the three-some I once had, which I'm pretty sure most people wouldn't consider a religious encounter. Well, maybe if it was a three-some with Pam Anderson and Denise Richards—that might qualify as a religious experience, but my three-some wasn't. The kind of faith I'm talking about is faith in yourself that really only comes from facing the things you're afraid of and getting through it. If you are scared enough times in your life, eventually you get to the point where you start to think, *"What's the worst that can happen? So I trip or faint or fail? Who cares?!?"* Then you start over and try again. Or you try something new. All the while, you're only getting better.

Failure is something I can deal with. Regret is not.

One time I wrote a blog post called *Are You Scared Shitless?* It was right after I gave a blind talk at Audience Conference. I mean, I had no PowerPoint, no notes, no panel. It was just me on a huge Broadway stage—with all the lights and velvet curtains and stuff—talking. And the audience was frickin' intimidating. I was talking to the executives from Ford, ABC News, Warner Brothers Records and guys like Jason Calacanis. Everyone in there was a heavy hitter and I decided to go off the cuff.

I have done a lot of stuff in my life, but I had never done THAT before.

Loren Feldman was the emcee that year and right before I went on he turned to me and said, "You nervous?"

"Shittin' bricks," is literally what I said because it sure felt like that in my stomach.

I believe that things die (like your creativity and your excitement) when you stay in your comfort zone. So you have to keep asking yourself— are you doing things that scare you shitless or are you happy to live in a comfort zone that is below your potential? That goes for work AND life.

I am constantly pushing myself in my work, whether it's giving a blind talk at a huge conference or starting a new venture. I am a revolutionary. And the thing is, well, revolutionary means doing something completely new and out-there. If everybody else is already doing it, it ain't new. And if no one is doing what you're doing, well then—you're all alone. You're taking a leap and that can be scary shit.

I have always done this in my life. I'm always leaping and I never know exactly where I'm going to land. But it's always an adventure, which brings us back to the story of how I met my wife.

Hold on because this one takes lots of turns.

Des Moines was such a contrast to my life in Moline. In general, there was just so much more energy—more jobs, restaurants, stores—that kind of stuff. But what I was really pumped about though, were the girls. There were so many more girls to access on Yahoo dating, it was like pink taco town and I was El Presidente, if you know what I mean.

Actually, there were too many for me to pay legit attention. I was a busy and pretty important man, let's not forget. I was revolutionizing Wells Fargo Financial by day and annihilating viruses, large and small, by night. All this left too little time to bait the many lovely ladies within my grasp.

So I did my thing. I wrote a script to spam every girl on Yahoo Dating within a 60 mile radius of my home base at George's. I figured that the odds were in my favor and that by principle of high volume alone I would get some quality response. As usual, I was right. I did not know just how consequential that spam would turn out to be in the big picture of my life.

Immediately, I got a ton of responses and had A LOT of casual fun around town. And then I got another email, Subject Line: PUSSYTROLLER. I opened it to find that this was not some kind of kinky request. It was a calling out. It read something like,

> *Dear Pussytroller,*
> *If you think you can just spam everyone and expect to meet anyone who would give you the time of day then you're a real asshole.*

I don't remember the rest of the email exactly. I'm not even sure I read the rest of it. I didn't have to. I already knew that I absolutely had to talk to this girl who was calling me out.

In my response I let my guard down completely, hoping she'd find some reason to carry on our exchange and stay in contact with me. I remember writing,

> *Look—I'm really not a bad guy. I'm not an asshole at all. In fact, I have really nice hands and I can give a great massage.*

That was God's honest truth, without any BS. It can't be denied that I do have really, very nice hands.

For some reason J wrote me back and we started chatting on the phone. That led to several nights of phone conversations until—without even realizing it—we started this pseudo relationship. I was dumbstruck by the feeling of intimate connection I felt to her. I don't mean intimate as in physical or sexual in any way. It wasn't like that. It was just an innocent connection—a feeling like you just know the other person in a way that is logically impossible. At this point we'd never met in person and yet I was more into J than any girl I had ever known in my life.

So then I learn that, not only is she ballsy enough to call me out on my BS, she was also beautiful and ridiculously smart. On top of all that, to me she sounded like that hardest working person on the face of the planet. When she was in high school she decided that she wanted a better education than she would get at the local public school so she worked two jobs to pay her way through private school. She worked her way through college at St John's in New Mexico and then got a scholarship for a progressive track within the business school at the University of Chicago. Because she realized in a summer pre-session that business wasn't the right fit for her, she re-grouped, re-tracked and got herself into medical school at University of Nebraska where she studied to become an anesthesiologist.

I was totally blown away by her. And here she was, talking to me. Wasting her time. I couldn't help but feel that way because in the back of my head that wiseass monkey was saying over and over again, "*You have nothing in common with this girl. Nothing in common with this girl. Nothing. She is way, way, WAY OUT OF YOUR LEAGUE. Move on!!!*" Oh, and also she was leaving Iowa in a few months anyhow, to complete her resident training in Omaha.

So, like a jackass, I hooked up with the easy chick instead. George had been trying to set me up with this girl named Melissa for a while. (Yes, another Melissa.)She was decent enough looking and I figured one date couldn't hurt. I mean, J and I had never met. I didn't think it was cheating or anything like that.

Everything about Melissa was easy. She wasn't super interesting or anything, but she was wild and spontaneous. We kind of spoke the same language. So right there, on our very first date we decided to move in together. I wanted to get out of George's hair and she had the room. When she threw it out there, it seemed like a quick fix to everything and an easy way to fall into a relationship. I had never really had one, after all. And here was this girl who was sweet and cute and fun, basically offering me everything.

In my head I had already decided that J wouldn't want me. Even though we had never met, and even though I was a little bit obsessed with her, I didn't think that it would work. Melissa was an immediate and easy alternative. J was intimidating. Melissa was comfortable. I chose Melissa.

J could smell my BS a mile away. I knew that she'd see through any excuse I gave her so when I called her up to explain my situation I told her the straight truth. I realized that it was strange to feel so connected and obligated to someone I had never even met in real life, but that's how it was. So I explained to her that I had met someone else and that —crazy as it seemed—we had gotten serious really quickly. I made sure to point out that she would be leaving soon anyhow and not pursuing our relationship any further was probably the smartest thing for us both.

If there was any physical way that I could have kicked myself in the ass with a steel toed boot the entire time I had her on the phone for our last conversation, I would have done it. I knew I was screwing up. And she was so cool. I remember her saying as casually as could be, "Don't worry about it. It's fine."

Regret is something you feel immediately. I felt it right then. I knew I was losing out on something amazing.

I wish my Spidey senses had been as sharp with Melissa. Maybe I did know that it wasn't going to work pretty early on and I just didn't listen because it was so easy at first. I mean—we me, we had sex and I got a new place to live, all in the first 24 hours. It was all win/win and everything was good for about two weeks. Unfortunately, that was also when we signed a TWO YEAR lease to live together. I had to know that was INSANE, but I did it anyway. I was like, "What's the worst that could happen?"

Well, in this case, the worst did happen and let me tell you, it was some messed up shit.

Maybe it's crossing the line telling you this next part but there is no way for you to get the picture without giving you the whole, juicy, explicit picture. Just don't let your kids read it. I mean, congratulations and everything that your kid is an honor student and a real bookworm, but what kind of parent are you? Put on a movie for them and keep reading. They don't need to know about any of this shit.

So, la-di-da. Everything was fine until the day Melissa asked me to fix her computer. In the process I noticed there was a CD in the drive. It was titled, "HOT PHOTOS & VIDEOS." Like any good boyfriend respecting his girlfriend's privacy, I opened it up immediately and started browsing. There were all these pictures of Melissa tied up and blindfolded. Then another girl showed up and she was tied up too. But this wasn't just any girl—it was Jen, her very cute best friend. Then came the pictures of them having sex and I'm like, "Whoa…..Okay. I can dig it." I knew Melissa was spicy and—whoa man, now we were talking. FANTASY LAND!

But then it started to take a different turn. Next came the pictures of Melissa having sex with tons of other guys—I'm talking gang bang. And then there were the kitchen utensils and people dressed up like animals and, well, I think you're starting to get the picture. I wasn't mad. I was just shocked. Maybe you're judging her right now, but honestly I did not care. Unless she was having sex that involved real live animals or children or using something gross like blood or poop, I didn't think it was wrong. In my mind, it just took her from a jalapeno to a habanero on the spicy scale.

But still, I was just shocked.

When she got home that night I talked to her about it. And wouldn't you know it—as it turned out her computer didn't need fixing at all (which was good, since I never got around to it). Her plan all along had been for me to find the CD. That was her way of telling me what she was into. She was too nervous to just tell me. She thought it would scare me away. But once the topic was opened and I didn't run away, she really opened up. She told me how she had been in love with Jen since they were both sixteen. Apparently, they had been sexually involved all along, lots of times sharing their boyfriends. By this time her friend was actually married and that worked into a threesome, from time to time.

And now here I was in the middle of everything. The next thing I know, Melissa tells me that Jen thought I was cute and together the two of them had been imagining a threesome with me. FUCK YEA. I mean, isn't this every guy's fantasy? It was definitely something I always wanted to add to my sexual resume, so I was fucking in.

I swear—Todd Phillips and the *Old School* dudes stole some of their material from me because the way it went down was a lot like when Mitch came home early from his conference. I came home from work and heard a bunch of moaning from the bedroom. I opened the door to find Jen all tied up, blindfolded and naked on the bed. Melissa was in between her legs—going to town and they pulled me right in.

I really don't know how to tell you what I need to say next. I don't know—maybe I need to turn in my man card, but I was totally disgusted by the whole thing. It's nauseating to watch someone you care about having passionate sex with another person. You can be all "FUCK YEA" at the start but then, once we were going, I just felt betrayed. Maybe it was because they started without me and then treated me like I was just a sideshow. I really don't know why. I only know that I felt hurt and then completely grossed out.

Wait for the freakin' bomb to drop…

The next night when I came home from work there was the moaning again. It was from the bedroom. I thought I knew what I was going to find when I opened the door and then BAM!

Melissa was passionately banging the husband.

So, I guess I forgot to declare THAT WAS NOT ALLOWED!

I was so pissed I started to throw my full weight at the guy. I wanted to tackle him and beat him half to death and then drop him over the balcony railing. But I stopped myself. I shut the door, grabbed a beer and sat on the couch. I flipped on the TV and turned the volume up to the max to drown out their screaming and moaning.

About ten minutes later—I shit you not—the guy walked out in his underwear. He helped himself to a beer and sat next to me on the couch. And then he was like, "Hey, how's it going? I am Mike, by the way—Jen's husband."

"*Yea. This is fucking awesome*," I thought to myself sarcastically. But out loud I was just like, "Doin' alright."

I believe in telling someone exactly what you need to as soon as you know what's up. Now, I didn't owe anything to Mike so I didn't tell him that he was one fucked up asshole. But that night I had to tell Melissa that there was no way I could live with this situation. I was surprised how upset she was. I mean a few hours before she was banging Mike, after all. I don't know. People are strange. We're all wired differently, I guess.

I couldn't sleep a wink that night. I was confused and pissed. I sat down at my computer and the only person I could think of was J. So I started to write her a long email, telling her everything. Well, not everything—just that I knew I had screwed up. I was living in the hell of my regret and I wanted to fix it. I wanted to go back and make a different choice. It poured out of me.

> *…The last thing I'm looking for is a relationship or even a date to be honest but we had so much fun talking I felt like I had such a good connection with you and I just want to be your friend. I just want to get a beer together sometime. I know you're leaving soon and I'm in this horrible relationship, but I just want to have a beer with you…*

She wrote me back the next day, something along these lines:

> *… Ok I guess. I felt like you ditched me before but if you really want to meet me so bad then you are welcome to come over. I live on the county hospital grounds in the doctor housing. I'm at home. I'm sick. I'm in my flannels and I'm watching the Westminster Dog Show. It's up to you. Come over it you want.*

That night I went to her house where she was, exactly as promised, in her flannels and we did, in fact, watch the dog show. I was so happy just to be there with her.

Oh, but I have to tell you about the smoking. At this point I had been a smoker for ten years. When I showed up I can only imagine how bad I smelled with ten years of stale smoke (plus the cigarette I just had in the car) hanging on me. But when you're a smoker, you don't notice. So there I was at her doorstep, the first time we ever met face-to-face and she is like, "Wait, under no condition can I date a smoker." And I was like, "I actually just quit today."

I don't know why she believed me and let me in, but she did. I followed her into her duplex and took a deep breath of fresh air as a new non-smoker. The cigarette I sucked down on the way to her house that night would, in fact, be the very last cigarette I would smoke for a very long time.

Great time for a quick departure from the story.

Side Note: The key to quitting smoking is actually very simple. It's not a magic bullet or a miracle pill. The key is replacement therapy. Screw off with your snide remark here. Smacking an itchy nicotine patch on your ass or gnawing down a pack of nicotine gum in between draws from a bottle of Captain Morgan could in fact be considered the magic bullets of nicotine replacement therapy (if, in fact they worked painlessly, which they don't). But I didn't say that the key is "nicotine replacement therapy." I said the key is simply "replacement therapy." If you replace your addiction with something that you want more, then the thing that you want more will win out and break your other addiction.

I wanted J more than anything. I realized that when she called me out as the *Pussy Troller*. I knew that the first time we talked for hours and hours on the phone. I couldn't push it away or replace it with a different relationship with an easy chick. I can't explain why or how but when she answered her door in her PJs she was the sexiest, most lovable and most irresistible thing I had ever encountered. I didn't even care that she had a prehistoric Gateway computer that stood five feet tall in the corner of her room. I couldn't help making fun of her relentlessly because of it, but that only added to the laughter that we shared. She cracked up right along with me because she knew who she was and didn't work to impress anyone.

J knew exactly who she was. She was strong, determined, beautiful and honest and I knew I wanted her more than anything I had ever wanted in my life. I needed to be with her.

There were more than a few obstacles to overcome, the least of which was that I was way, way—a fucking galaxy-wide way—out of my league to start. Assuming that I could get J to see beyond that and want to be with me as much as I wanted to be with her, I still had some problems. I mean, I wasn't exactly in a courting position. I had a girlfriend who liked all sorts of crazy sexual shit and I lived with her. I had just made some big mistakes and I was scared to make another mistake, even though I was living in Hell. The whole thing was a mess.

That's just what I thought.

Actually, life is really just a matter of perspective. If you think you can't fix something—you can't. If you think you can't change something—you won't. But if you can muster the courage to take a leap of faith, you will end up someplace new. In one case you might end up living with a crazy nymphomaniac and feeling really shitty about yourself. In another case you might end up moving next door to your soul mate.

But you can't waste a bunch of time thinking about it, especially when you're talking about a girl.

Every guy knows that there is this thing called the girlfriend window. It's a simple concept. When you meet a girl, if you start as friends, there is a short and non-negotiable amount of time in which you can move the relationship from friendly to romantic. J called me The *Pussy Troller* sometime in September of 2001 and we were now in early February. Even with a brief disconnect in the middle of our friendly conversations, I was very aware that I was working against a fast closing girlfriend window. I knew we had to go out on a real I-want-YOU date, like pronto.

So, I asked and she said yes.

I picked her up that night in my "chick-magnet"—a tan Ford Astrovan that topped out at 50 mph. It wasn't much to look at or to ride in, but I wanted it, at least, to be clean. So I spent all afternoon scrubbing it, like until my knuckles were bleeding. Still, it reeked like a bowling alley ashtray that hadn't been emptied since 1979.

I rolled up and J was dressed to the nines. Seriously, she was smokin'. (You know what I mean, not literally). She was hot and I was in my track suit in an Astrovan that stunk. When she climbed in she looked at me all suspicious and I had to tell her again, "Honest to God, I quit." That was fact.

The other fact was that I had twenty bucks in my pocket. I'm not really sure what I was thinking. If you haven't figured it out by now, I'm not much of a planner. I just take my chances. At this point, I had a shot with J and I took it. The first thing she did was order a $20 pitcher of margaritas.

Oh, shit. That didn't go so hot.

You see, the thing wasn't just that I was short of cash in my pocket. I was short of money, period. I didn't even have a checkbook. When you are tens of thousands of dollars in debt to several credit card companies, establishing a new bank account is not something you can easily do. I was literally scraping dollars together while I was in my first few months at WFF in Des Moines and twenty was all I had for the romantic big date. I'm thinking all of this while J is—I'm not making this up—telling me stories about this loser guy she had dated for a short time while I was getting screwed over by Melissa. Apparently, he never had any cash either and he only lasted two dates.

That's when I just blurted out with it. "So, I got 20 bucks in my pocket and you just ordered a $20 margarita pitcher."

We ate a few chips. I was silently willing my superhero powers to produce an AmEx Black Card in my pocket. The waitress poured our margaritas and J started laughing. She was like, "Don't worry about it," and we both started cracking up—like the kind of laughing when you might snort salsa out of your nose.

It was an amazing night. That's my kind of love story. I think true love means being with someone who you can really laugh with and completely lose your shit. It's being with someone who just loves you for you even when you're at your worst with twenty bucks to your name. Simple as that.

We still love that story to this day and tell it at dinner parties until the entire table loses their shit in laughter. In fact, the $20 margarita is one of our all-time favorite stories, followed closely, by the time when I was too scared to take off my pants (in bed), which came a few dates later.

When I was with J I felt the oddest combination of opposite feelings. Every time we were together, all at once I felt completely comfortable but also totally fucking petrified like a scared little bitch. I would listen to her talk about how her sister built this phone booth company and then started a huge horse ranch and how her brother was a bigwig for EDS. And here she was, about to become an anesthesiologist and make shittons of cabbage and I was like, "Yeah. You know. I'm doin'…okay…too…" even though, in comparison, I hadn't achieved close to what these people had. But the thing about being with J was that she made me feel like I could do whatever I wanted. I never felt bad about myself, in comparison, she just made me feel like there was so much potential in my future.

Still, I was scared shitless. I didn't have a history with girls. I didn't know what I was supposed to do next when you are really falling in love with someone. After a few dates all we had done was kiss a lot.

Then one night at her doorstep I kissed her good night and started walking away but she was like, "Do you want to come in and lay down with me?" And I'm like, "Uhhhh....YES!" I took her hand and followed her inside. We lay down together and started totally making out for a while until she stopped all of a sudden and was like, "Wait...Do you still have your PANTS ON?!?!"

Well, of course I did. I was a scared little bitch. I didn't know what I was supposed to do. I had nothing really to draw from, except for the crazy hoes I had been with who attacked me. I didn't know how to take control and what was appropriate.

It's hilarious now, but at the time my face was probably purple with shame. Actually it's only hilarious now because at the time she didn't care and she didn't find me stupid or scared and she didn't laugh at me. J just saw me being me and we kissed and laughed together. And yes, she kept her arms around me until I took my pants off.

I have been told I can exaggerate the truth sometimes. Well then, let me say that this is no exaggeration just so we're clear. Without J, I would be dead. I would be dead for a number of reasons and bad decisions.

I could have ended up exactly like my friend Bryce. Our lives were nearly identical for a while. I met him in a random chat room late at night when only the tech geeks are awake and staring at a computer screen. We both practically lived online. We were both obsessive smokers and practically alcoholics. Did I mention we were also both morbidly obese? We both came from the Quad City area. When I got my job at WFF and began to rule the company I convinced Bryce to follow my footsteps and got him hired as a system administrator under my supervision. At one point we even had 1 BR apartments in the same complex.

Then I met J.

Shortly after, Bryce died in his sleep from a drunken stroke.

I really miss him even now. He was a great friend. He had very little boundaries when it came to political correctness, which probably stemmed from his addiction to South Park. I only tell you this because at his funeral the priest was this young Asian guy who kept pronouncing his name as "Blice." He would have laughed his ass off at that. I hope he was watching.

My point is that even if I knew in advance that I would 100% end up dying in my sleep just like Bryce, if it hadn't been for J, I am sure that I would NOT have made the decision that I needed to make to save my life. Without J, I would never have agreed to undergo a duodenal switch that the doctors promised would reduce my weight by nearly half and instantly cure my diabetes and according to WFF human resources, was also fully covered by my insurance plan. This procedure is the closest thing in the world to the existence of a magic bullet or miracle pill and I would never have taken the leap if J wasn't by my side.

I was scared shitless to be put under anesthesia—for good reason.

Ready for a flashback? (Oh, I also have to add that in the movie version this next scene is going to be so awesome. The make-up people could be nominated for some type of award for making my leg look as torn up as it was with all the fat sticking out of it. God, movies are the best.)

I was in seventh grade hanging with my buddies, Eric Collins and Todd Whiting doing time trials on our dirt bikes. During my turn I was doing well and making really good time. Then I hit a jump and crashed. When I went to get up I couldn't. Something felt really strange. I looked down in horror to see my handlebar stuck INSIDE of my leg. It had ripped a hole in my leg from just below my groin to just above my knee.

It's funny that I couldn't actually move *until* I saw my leg busted open. One look at my leg and my adrenaline spiked. I shot up to my feet and started screaming and wildly running around in circles. I was running and running and running while that voice in my head said on repeat, *"I'm dead. I'm dead. This is being dead. I'm dead. I'm dead. This is being dead."*

Todd was no help. He just kept puking over and over again on his own shoes. But Eric was another story. He was fucking money. I have no idea how he knew this shit, I think his mom was a nurse or something. He ripped off his sweatshirt and tied it around the top of my leg, really tight like a tourniquet. At some point an ambulance got there and rushed me to the ER. By this time I had gone into shock.

All I can remember is hearing the word "amputation" and nothing else. I was 250 pounds of crazy with no idea what was happening or where I was. All I knew was that if I completely lost consciousness I was going to end up with no right leg. Somehow I busted out of my restraints and pulled out the tubes and needles and even punched someone. When the nurses tried to hold me down I pushed them off like a crazed lunatic. There were so many people on top of me I felt like I was suffocating and losing this fight that I just couldn't lose.

The last thing I remember was the gas mask on my face and the horrific feeling that I was suffocating. I can't describe the panic I felt and it's hard to understand unless it happens to you—your lungs screaming for air. It's the scariest feeling I have ever had, well—except for the thing with my daughter, but I'm getting way ahead of myself.

At this point what I want to say is *Thank you, Eric Collins for saving my leg.* Because of him and his sweatshirt tourniquet the doctors didn't have to amputate. I woke up with a two foot scar on my leg and went through a bitch of a recovery. The wound was so deep it took months to actually close up. I used to charge kids a buck for a peek under my bandage so they could see what the inside of a leg looks like. That was cool. But the feeling of being suffocated, I never forgot that. I had nightmares about it and swore I would never go under anesthesia again.

Fast forward nineteen years and I fall in love with an anesthesiologist. That's irony if I have ever fucking heard of it.

With J I was happier than I had ever been, but physically I was reaching a breaking point. I had a sleep study done, which showed that during the night I stopped breathing for a 180 seconds. I'll do the math for you. That's a full three minutes. That's not healthy. So they gave me an oxygen tank like an 80 year old man and when I slept I had to strap the CPAP mask on my face. When I was diagnosed with diabetes J was like, "Enough. You can't live like this."

She did a ton of research to present me with the facts of the procedure and went through the whole process with me. I have to say that she made a damn good case. Between that and the promise that she would be in the OR the entire time, monitoring my status, I agreed to have the duodenal switch.

162

I can't tell you how much I weighed at my heaviest because I didn't have access to a freight scale. On the day of my surgery, however, I officially weighed 420 pounds (but this was after the required thirty day extreme fast that you have to do to loosen up your flab and make it easier for the doctors to get in there). I guess the numbers don't really matter after all. 420, 440, 460. Whatever the number, I was fat. I was dying of fat until J convinced me to face my fear of anesthesia. I had the surgery and I can tell you that a few months after, with a regular diet and normal exercise, I weighed in at 170 pounds. A year later I was at a healthy and maintainable 200. That's where I have stayed—alive and well.

So after all of that—here's my point again. Sometimes you just have to take a leap of faith and ask yourself, "What's the worst thing that can happen?" If you're not scared shitless, you're probably too comfortable and if you're too comfortable you're not living the life you could be living. I can live with failure. I can live with everyone reading this crazy stuff about my life and laughing at me. I can live with embarrassment and ridicule and fear.

I will not live with regret.

14

Parting Out and Cashing In

As long as you're going to be thinking anyway, think big.

-DONALD TRUMP

Eventually I was fired from Wells Fargo. I found a way to automate my job and get all my work done with 100% efficiency. And for that type of thinking—smart and efficient—I was fired.

But I guess I need to back up a little bit.

I made the job at Wells Fargo sound pretty kick ass before and a lot of it was. I loved the puzzle-type stuff like messing around with viruses and I also actually liked training the staff. But my primary task everyday was super boring. It was my job, along with two other colleagues, to go through hundreds of pages of data entry logs and look for anomalies. And while mining for anomalies might sound like sexy spy work to you, let me be clear so that you understand how awful this was.

I manually reviewed every transaction from each teller at every WFF branch across the country. I would get a stack of printed reports that were each between 6 and 8 inches thick and I had to look through every code on every line of every page and look for anything that was out of place. If I found something suspicious—which happened maybe once in 50,000 lines—then I'd highlight it and initial it. Once I finished I would take that report and pass it to one of the other senior members of the security team to be double checked and they would give me theirs, in exchange. This is what the three of us did most of the day, every day.

Dumb.

Why would I spend my valuable time and creative energy on something so ridiculous and so easily automated? Right?! Why should I play according to the rules when the rules are gay and the people who make the rules are retarded? I knew I could find a quicker way. One night I wrote a script to review the lines for me. What used to take 3 hours, then took me 10 minutes. Using my script I had 100% accuracy and a shitload of new free time.

You've have heard of Wells Fargo, right? It's a big commercial brand bank. Like any commercial brand they liked everything to be standardized and uniform—policies, processes, letterheads and equipment. When they acquired small local banks or renovated existing branches, they would do an infrastructure house cleaning and because I was on the security team, I was always sent to oversee the process and make sure that all the equipment was disposed of properly. If we were dealing with old Wells Fargo hard drives those would be sent to a facility for incineration to ensure that all sensitive information was destroyed. But with all the other infrastructure and non-WF hard drives we called in a technology recycling company called Redemtech. The pick-up was a free service and WFF got a small percentage of any future resale.

Over time I got to be buddies with the Redemtech dudes since I would see them on a weekly basis at these haul-aways. Eventually we kind of ran out of things to talk about so one day I was like, "What the hell do you guys do with all this junk?" The thing is that most people only think about the stuff they see right in front of their faces. Most people aren't curious about what happens behind the interface of a computer or what happens to their garbage after they throw it in the trash. But I was interested because I watched crap loads of hardware "disappear" on a pretty regular basis.

It wasn't just because I was curious. I knew there was a business model there and I wanted to understand it. One of my buddies gave me his login credentials so I could get into Redemtech's internal website and nose around and this is what I found. Redemtech had an incredible inventory. There were all these computers, which I knew were basically brand new because I had just ripped them out of the wall personally. That part was great, but what was amazing was that these computers were resold by the truckload. Now I've already established that I'm not an outdoors kind of guy, certainly not an agriculture dude. But looking at computers like this only made me think of crops. It was like buying soybeans or cornmeal or some shit.

Yes, Hi. I'll take 1,000 pounds of Dell hard drives and throw in another 600 pounds of IBM monitors. Thank you.

I wasn't exactly sure what this opportunity was or how I would flesh it out, but I definitely knew this was an angle. I only had two problems: capital and storage. Okay, so those are kind of big problems, but they just made the whole thing more fun—like more of a puzzle to figure out and put together. I was still ridiculously in debt, but I figured if I could just get the cash for the first lot, everything would work itself out. I needed exactly $2,000. That would buy a lot of something like a couple hundred computers, which brings us to the second problem. Assuming you don't have your very own warehouse, where would you store 2-300 computers? Well, I didn't have a warehouse, but lucky for me I was in love with a beautiful, smart, capable and **understanding** woman. Through J, I solved both problems.

J had just moved into this little house outside of Omaha near the hospital where she was completing her residency. Every weekend I would drive out there from Des Moines so we could spend time together. One weekend I told her about my idea and as you can imagine she was not really into it. In fact I think she actually called it "gambling." I started to explain risk and odds to her, but then I remembered something about picking your battles. So I just agreed that I could see how my idea looked risky from the outside, but from my perspective, it was a no-brainer. I was like, "Just trust me on this one. Oh, and I also need to use your house as the headquarters/warehouse for this new 'small business.'" She wasn't exactly thrilled, but she did agree. I think she mostly went along with it at the beginning because she had no clue how I was going to cough up the startup money to buy all these computers.

But I had an idea. I was going to ask her mom for a loan. I know most people loathe their mother-in-laws but Susan is a gem and she has always been my biggest supporter. (Yep, I said "gem.") Low and behold, she totally came through with five grand. It came with a promissory note, which tied J to the loan by stating that if I didn't pay the money back it would come directly out of her share of the inheritance in her mom's will. It was a smart contingency by her mom, especially considering this crazy boyfriend of her daughter's was about to start slinging raw computer parts from a lawn in the Omaha ghetto, even if I was so fucking lovable.

The look on J's face when she read that clause was PRICELESS. She realized she was about to not only house my new venture, but also to fund it. I told you she was quite a woman. ;)

I should clear up any misunderstanding that you have about J's background here. She was not a silver spoon kid. Her parents went through a very bad divorce in which her brother and sister suffered a ton. All that stuff is really her business and she's not the one putting everything out there and public in a book so let's just leave it by saying she had a tough time growing up. Because of that, J learned to be very conservative with money—to spend it on the things that mattered most, like education, and save anything else then you can manage at the end of the day.

So if you consider their background, for J and for her mom this angle was a gamble, I suppose. I didn't see it that way though. They gave me the money and I immediately bought my first lot. I paid $2,000 and I got 250 computers. By parting out each computer and re-selling the individual components on eBay I did really well. That very first truckload I tripled my money. I paid back J's mom immediately and was off to the cash races.

I could leave the story as simple as that. But I won't. Because then you won't learn anything. You see, my point isn't just to brag here about how cool and smart and handy I can be. The point is to remind you how much effort it takes to make it big. Of course you need to start by thinking big, but then you have to back up the ideas with good old fashioned time and sweat. Too often we all sit around with our thumbs up our asses waiting for a settlement or a winning lottery ticket or an inheritance from a long-lost great aunt to cash rescue us from our problems. A few lucky ones get to live out this fantasy, but the majority of us (myself included) have no choice but to work for what we get.

Let's review.

1. I was successful because I was willing to do what others were willing not to do.
2. I saw an angle and took it immediately and aggressively because I knew it wouldn't last long (as they never do).
3. I worked my ass off.

And that's the gist if you want the short version.

But there's more to it.

Because I had automated most of my responsibilities at Wells Fargo, I spent most of my time at work shopping online for computers at Redemtech. I also wouldn't share my program with anyone else on the security team, which led to some resentment, but that's a whole 'nother story. (I'll put the tangent in a parenthesis this time: The moral of that story is that it really is better to share your shit than to be a selfish jerk. It leads to less hassle, anyhow.) At the end of each week I would drive two and a half hours from Des Moines to Omaha and pull up to J's house on Friday night just as the Redemtech dudes were finishing unloading all my stuff. I hope you have the right picture in your head right now. It was hilarious to look at—hundreds of crates full of hardware and wires, stacked up onto this tiny little lawn in the ghetto of Omaha. Thank god, J was working like a dog and was never around to see it. That would not have been so hilarious.

Another relaxing Saturday.

The other thing, which wasn't hilarious at all, was how endless those days seemed. After the drive I would jump out of my car and start carrying the computers into the house one after another, after another.

This would go on until about 2 or 3 am, just about the time that J was probably looking for a back room at the hospital to crash in. The next job was to dissemble everything with a screwdriver into individual components. You see, the market for whole used computers isn't huge. There are enough deals around that the average American can afford to buy a new computer. There was a market for the individual parts, though. I saw that right away, so I parted out most every computer in my Redemtech lots. Well, eventually the neighbor kid was the one who actually did the dissembling. I paid him five bucks an hour, which I considered a great use of cash.

Since I was dealing with pretty much the same exact computer, with a small variation in model and year, I was essentially building an inventoried warehouse of Dell computer parts. At that point I could tell you the going rate of every part and button. I had templates set up on eBay and priced each accordingly over time as I learned. Some computers would sell whole once I learned which models mattered. But the thing was that it never mattered to my buyers which hard drives were in them, so long as there was a hard drive. So again, as I learned, I increased my profits. I would buy lots of the whole selling computers and huge lots of shitty hard drives. I would swap the good RAM out of the whole computers, replace them with the shitty RAM for a complete product and then turn around and sell the good RAM individually.

I did that every weekend for six months and made a good deal of cash, enough to dig myself out of debt and start living as a not-completely-financially fucked degenerate. I saw an angle and I took it. It was risky and not glamorous AT ALL. I was willing to do what others were willing not to do and because of that I had the advantage—but only for a while.

All good angles close with time and this was no exception. After the first six months the inventory slowed while companies much bigger than my front lawn Omaha shop began to outbid me for the big lots.

So I retired from the computer part business while things were still looking up for me. I had learned enough by that point to know that hanging your hat on one and only one opportunity is never smart. You hang on long enough to ride the big wave and then cut out before it gets dicey and desperate. I'm always okay with retiring from something. That's because I always know there is another angle around the corner for me to find.

I still had time after all. I had lots and lots of time to fuck around when I didn't have to do my real job anymore (because it was already mechanically and perfectly being done for me). So when I didn't have to shop for computer inventory anymore I started messing around with my new, cool phone.

It wasn't just any phone; it was a Nextel phone—you know, the ones that go *chirp chirp*. All my friends had the same phone and we'd *chirp chirp* back and forth all the time in the way that you could radio each other. I loved that phone and you know me, I'm no average consumer. I needed to understand everything about the phone and how it worked.

One day I was on this Nextel forum learning about how to hack into the phone so I could wire it to a case that flashed when I got incoming calls. This is right when color screens first came out on phones so I also wanted to pimp my phone out with a picture of my hot girlfriend. As I hit the Internet to figure out how to do this, I realized that it was actually going to be a bit tricky. For example, there were only so many colors you could use when you formatted the image. Also you had to doctor it up exactly to the right pixel dimension and the file size had to match within a few small bytes. If that was not difficult enough, at the time IBM had a patent on the GIF format so there were not any formatting tools available for free. Unless you were someone with a lot of software lying around and a lot of time to screw around, you would probably give up.

I had both the software and the time (plus I'm really stubborn). So, of course, I figured it out. But it took a few minutes and certainly wasn't easy. As soon as I finished getting J's pic on my phone I wrote a complete how-to guide for formatting and uploading GIF images to Nextel phones. I published it on a place called Howard Forums and still, people couldn't seem to figure it out on their own. Since my name and contact information was on the forum, I began to get direct requests from people wanting me to reformat their images for them. I had no problem with that. It was fun until I started to get between fifty and a hundred emails a day. That was overload.

Need is the mother of invention, right? There's a saying like that because it's true. I didn't want to give up this challenge, but I absolutely needed a more efficient process of reformatting. So I wrote a program to do it automatically. I happened to own the domain name bigbootiehoes.com and I wasn't using it for anything at the time so I just put the script on that website. Tons of people started using it, like thousands per day. About a month later someone suggested that I rename the site or at least get a different domain because evidently some people don't know how to proxy tunnel out and when they surf to websites named bigbootiehoes.com their employers don't like it.

He had a point though. And this site was getting A LOT of action. People were converting tens of thousands of images a day for their Nextel phones. Out of nowhere, one day the name just came to me: *NextPimp*. It was so obvious. The site was about pimping out your Nextel Phone and becoming the Next Pimp. I guess that wasn't exactly a huge upgrade as far as the idiots who don't know how to proxy tunnel out of a questionable website were concerned, but I didn't care. It was my site and I was offering a really valuable service to anyone—for free. All you had to do was upload a picture in any size and format and the program would resize it correctly and spit it out as a zip file that could be uploaded by any numbskull onto their Nextel phone.

I didn't stop there.

The real success factor for any new idea or invention is whether you can take the original prototype designed for a specific and limited audience and then diversify the concept for everyone in a way that doesn't cheapen or de-purpose the original idea. I decided to expand past Nextel and have a program on the site that worked for each of the popular cell phones on the current market. That was obvious to me. But what didn't occur to me was that while I was offering my visitors this free service I could also be building a legit inventory of wallpaper images. Again, you have to remember that this is pre-YouTube and before clouds and the idea that user traffic can collectively build up an inventory of anything.

It didn't occur to me until one day when someone pointed out that I was doing all this work, but I wasn't taking the few extra steps to save and categorize all the images that users were uploading. People were, after all, mostly uploading images of their favorite musical artists or celebrities—stuff that other users would be interested in accessing as well. Now we know this process of cataloguing as "tagging," but at that time there was no term for it. I can't exactly say that I knew how big this would become; I just thought it was a really cool idea. So I started saving and cataloguing the images as we went. As my users began to upload thousands of images a day a massive inventory of wallpapers began to develop.

At work I was REALLY busy, just not so much with my job. I was really busy building and supporting NextPimp and thinking up ways to get myself from Des Moines to Omaha to be with J. Sure I ran the occasional staff meeting but that only took about an hour a week. In time my bosses noticed that I wasn't quite as focused as the other guys in my security group (rats) and I got fired. At least that solved my relocation issue.

Since I had wanted to get to Omaha anyhow I had put out a few resumes to different banks here and there and one of the hungry bites I got was from a bank called Commercial Federal in downtown Omaha. NextPimp wasn't a revenue source for me and knowing that I was going back to a life within a bank (starting a job that I had already conquered and would more-than-likely be full of mind-numbing responsibilities) I decided, at least, to negotiate a salary that would excite me. You always negotiate when you know the buyer is hungry and I knew Commercial Federal really wanted me because of my experience and credentials. Even though I was only making $42K a year at WFF, I told them I was pulling in $80K. They gritted their teeth and reached deep in their pockets to be able to offer me $78,000 in salary. I gave them an *uggghhhhh-well-I-really-want-to-be-there-so-I-guess-I'll-to-make-do* acceptance and moved my ass to sweet Nebraska and in with J.

Commercial Federal was nothing out-of-the-box. They wanted me to do exactly what I had done at WFF (minus the part where I wrote the script to do my job even better than I could ever do my job, without doing my job). So I wrote new security policies for them and led the security training, but since I still had the original copy I wrote for WFF I wasn't exactly starting from scratch. And again I breezed through my daily work life. Honestly, I have decided, that most of any office job is getting really good at the art of acting like you're busy. I had no problem with that. I sat in front of my computer for hours, totally focused and busy—just not on bank stuff.

This was a year after I originally started NextPimp and at this point, ringtones were just starting to roll out.

NextPimp had become the go-to site for people to format and customize images for their phones. I didn't see any reason why I couldn't do the same thing for ringtones, on the exact same model. Naturally, NextPimp also became the go-to site for anyone to upload a song in any format or length and turn it into a ringtone. Yep, my programs would format the file and chop it up into a pretty little downloadable version for any kind of phone.

It was brilliant and legit and it grew like crazy wild fire.

Not only was my site the only one of its kind, I also understood search engine optimization (SEO) so I was ranking #1 for everything: ringtones, free ringtones, Tupac ringtones, best ringtones. I also had access to real-time keyword data from inside my site. That's when I realized that bidding and controlling the misspelled versions of keywords can be really helpful too. (You have no idea how much traffic I have gotten from Tuppac spelled with two "P"s and that's just one example.) Anyhow, my traffic was out of control. As we approached the peak, people were uploading 35,000 files per day.

The irony was that while the site was absolutely killing it, I wasn't making a single dime. It was my obsession, but it was a free service. I wanted to make it the best possible service it could be and my pay-out was counting the crap loads of users I was getting. It was a pride thing, I guess—pride in my work and pride in the popularity of my idea. Pride doesn't pay the electric bill though, and an obsession takes time.

As it turned out, I wasn't quite as good at looking like I was busy with bank stuff while I was busy working on my own shit as I thought I was and eventually the axe came down. I got fired from yet another gig.

In June 2005, I went on unemployment while I tried to figure out my next move. I didn't really have many prospects, just this kick ass site that was getting hundreds of thousands of mobile users a day. A few weeks later the phone rang.

The woman on the line was like, "Are you Jeremy Schoemaker, the owner of NextPimp.com?"

And I was like, "Yes."

She went on to tell me, "I work for this company called Google…" and then she barreled into everything.

They had noticed how much mobile traffic I was getting for ringtones. This was interesting to them because they had a ton of inventory to advertise to my specific traffic through their AdSense program. According to their reports, she told me I would qualify for their premium revenue share program. My broke ass could only think of one important question: How much could I make from this revenue share program? As a "guestimate," she threw out a couple of conservative numbers but they were good enough to keep me interested in trying this out. Something was better than nothing at this point, I figured. I knew how to get the traffic and I knew that had to be worth something. I just didn't know how to make it into something on my own.

On that very first phone call the chick walked me through the process and I was enrolled in AdSense. We set up my account, I copied and pasted the code into my site and I was up and running Google sponsored ads to the hundreds of thousands of unique (and unsolicited) visitors that NextPimp had daily.

I never exaggerate when I talk about money. When I say that I hadn't made a single dime from NextPimp to this point, I mean I didn't make a dime or a dollar or a penny. Nothing. And when I say that immediately after setting up my AdSense account with Google, I was making thousands a day, I mean that the very day after I hung up with the Google chick I made $1,500 and somewhere between $1,000-8,000 per day, every day in the first few months. Literally. No exaggeration.

The first pay-out check that arrived from Google to our Omaha mailbox was for $132, 994.97. Subtracting the expense of one server and the hosting cost of $299, every remaining penny was my personal profit. It was a very good first month.

Still, I couldn't actually cash in my millions of dimes. Remember, I was still on unemployment and my finances hadn't exactly been in order— ever. When I walked into my local Wells Fargo branch and presented my check to the teller she looked at me like, what the hell is going on here?! I had bounced four checks from the same account in the previous month and now here I was with this game show sized check from this Google company. The teller said to me, "I don't know whether to call out the president to shake your hand or call in the police." That's an exact quote.

They held the check for 90 days. Just to be sure that I was for real.

In the meantime I was becoming the poster boy for Google's AdSense program, traveling around giving little talks here and there about how to cash in on the opportunity. I had attended Digital Point forums since 2003 through which I had a small following already. I'm the kind of guy who's hard to ignore, especially in person and most especially when I'm talking about all the crazy ways I have found to make money. And since that time, on the advice of one of my groupies, I began writing a little-read blog called Shoemoney.com. I wrote it like no one would ever read it. My posts were blunt and crass and riddled with horrible grammar from the start. I was only interested in being 100% myself and chronicling my crazy adventures. I never intended for my blog or me personally to become the authority on Internet marketing. That's just how it played out.

After I saw how AdSense paid out, I kept climbing the ladder upwards, trying to find greater and greater sources of money. I followed the money and ended up in an affiliate network. I was in the right place at the right time with an incredibly valuable site. That's when the profits skyrocketed to several hundred thousand dollars per month and I was on pace to become a millionaire in no time.

That's the part that everyone remembers when they hear my story. Jeremy became a millionaire overnight. It's a real-life rags to riches story if that's how you see it. But in my eyes, this was thirty years in the making—through my failures and my bankruptcy and the lessons I learned on each crazy turn in the road. In my eyes, I was still a guy without a degree and a real grown-up job, who happened to be cashing in on an angle that probably wouldn't last much longer.

Maybe you see a millionaire—a lucky, cocky, bastard.

But I see an underdog who works every day from the ground up, one part at a time, to build things he thinks have value. I see a guy who thinks big, but has no Ivory Tower. I see a guy who likes to cash in when it's time to cash in, but knows—more often than not—he needs to work harder. I see a guy who's willing to do what others are willing not to do because he knows that it pays off.

In the late months of 2005 in our little house in Omaha I was becoming a millionaire. But every day I was looking for a real day job, because there was still a little self-conscious voice inside me preaching that was the thing to do.

15

Buy a Good Bed, Marry a Good Woman
(And Get Your Potholders at Target)

When you accept the impossible you start to find solutions.

-Me, JEREMY R. SCHOEMAKER

I skipped over the part where J and I got married because I didn't want to bury an important story like that in the middle of a story about making piles of money. This isn't to say that the part about making ridiculous piles of money isn't important because, let's be real people—money is important. It's so important that I'll quote the *Boiler Room* boys again. "They say money can't buy happiness? Look at the fucking smile on my face. Ear to ear, baby."

Money is good. Money can buy happiness and $132,994.97 checks always make me smile. But money is made to be spent—to come and go and buy lots of cars and toys and diamonds and shit. My wife is with me forever and that makes me smile in a different way, like a deeper and more essential happiness that is from ear to ear but also down in my heart where I didn't even know it was possible to smile before I met her.

Wait, I just thought of something else I have to tell you so I gotta' pause quickly. (Then I'll get back to the lovey dovey stuff.)

People are funny. It's funny how they cheap out. I have spent a lot of time understanding who buys what and how and when. As an Internet marketer, I have to understand that stuff. One thing I can say for sure is that everyone always wants a deal. People will spend hours on end looking for a deal that might save them twenty bucks. People will compromise on the really important shit in order to save a little money. I, however, am not like that so let me give you two pieces of advice here.

First, know the value of your time. I know that I've already said that a bunch of times and you'll probably hear it from me another time before we're done because it's so important. I paid sticker price for the last car I bought. The single reason I did this was because my time is worth a lot more when I'm in the office working than if I'm saving 2 grand haggling over the price of the car. Some people might call me a chump for at least not trying, but I call it smart. I can't afford to waste my precious time like that. Secondly, don't be cheap out on the important stuff. I spend most of my life in my computer chair and in my bed. So I bought the top of the line Herman Miller Aeron and a pimped out Sleep Number mattress. Again, to me, that's just smart. I want my ass to be happy.

A comfortable chair, a good bed and an awesome wife. That's a perfect recipe for happiness. Everything else you can take in stride and figure out, even if it's stuff that seems impossible at the time.

Take my wedding for example.

When I asked my wife to marry me, I had a whole different wedding in mind. I proposed on Thanksgiving in 2003 with the plan to get married on the first of January in neon, romantic Las Vegas. I was thrilled that J said yes, but less thrilled and more confused by her terms. Yes I was the guy for her. Yes she was ready to be engaged. Yes she was excited to get used to the idea of being engaged and to imagine everything she wanted her wedding to be. She just needed a little time to adjust and for me to understand that NO WAY IN HELL WAS HER WEDDING GOING TO BE IN VEGAS.

Okay, so marriage is supposed to be about compromise. Yin and yang. Two people who come together not as mirror images but like puzzle pieces. I got that and I forfeited all the ideas of the wedding in my mind so we could do it like J wanted. All that really mattered to me anyways was marrying her. What did I care about the flowers and colors and shit?!

I gotta' say that people get too hung up on looking at the world how they think it should be and not just as it is. We come up with imaginary rules about what is possible and impossible in our lives, making really important decisions according to these rules. I'm no exception. For most of my life I thought it was impossible for me to not be really fat. I thought it wasn't possible to be legitimately successful without a college degree. I also thought there was no way I'd ever get laid, let alone married, which meant it was very impossible for me to ever be a dad. I thought about that stuff once in a while. But mostly I just centered my decisions on the very real possibility that I would be dead before turning 30.

Shows how much I know.

Scratch that.

Shows how much I *knew*.

This is my point. If you can accept what everyone else sees as impossible and get outside of those imaginary boundaries, you don't have to have a cape to fly. That in itself is a pretty fucking awesome superhuman power.

Location, colors, menu. Whatever. The only reason I can think of that anyone would let this crap worry them is so that the mind is distracted from the scary fucking shadow of the really big wedding issue. As we planned and set a date and got closer to our May 2004 wedding (which was definitely not taking place in Vegas) I got more and more nervous and just plain old scared as shit. The concept is scary, you have to admit.

You stand there and swear to another person that you'll be in it with her forever and ever. I don't even know what the fuck "forever" means and I'm not talking about my reading comprehension issues here. I'm talking about a concept that is beyond human experience. What have you or I ever experienced that is "forever?" I tell you what: absolutely nothing. So then, I ask you, not if forever is possible or impossible, but just how can understanding forever or promising forever be possible? The answer is: I have no fucking idea. But you just have to do it. When you accept the impossible (or the impossible to understand) you start to see solutions and possibilities and happiness that you never imagined before.

Now there's a happy guy!

I accepted that J and I would figure out what forever meant and I accepted the unbelievable fact that this incredible woman loved me for who I was. She believed in me and my potential. That made a big difference. That was my course correction in a very *Adjustment Bureau* kind of a way.

This doesn't mean that marriage is a no-brainer as soon as you say "I do." Marriage is hard work and I don't think it would be possible, at all, if you don't respect one another above everything else. J and I do it all. We fight, we disagree and we compromise when it's necessary but at the end of the day I listen to her because she has the chops to back up her ideas.

Everyone loves to talk at you. I've been lectured by hundreds of people in my past about what I should or shouldn't be doing but these opinions mean nothing to me if the loose-lippers don't have the experience to back up their advice. J does. She's got it all. I have seen how much she's studied and worked for the things that she wants and that makes me listen to her even when I really frickin' don't want to.

For J life is easy. I don't mean that as lazy or dumb-lucky. I mean easy like simple and straight forward. Maybe clinical is a better word. But the problem with that is it sounds like she's cold and sterile or even uppity. She's not. She's warm and compassionate and generous, but she doesn't get overly emotional when it's better to be analytical. For example, J wanted a really good education so she calculated the cost, got a few jobs and a lot of loans and put herself through private high school and college. She didn't complain herself into a dead-end. She found her best way through. Then when she decided to become a doctor she calculated the cost and made the grades and worked as hard as she needed to reach her goal. Recently she wanted to run a marathon so she joined a running group and followed the running program and built up enough strength to finish the race. For J, life is easy like *that*. She never thinks anything she wants is impossible. She knows it just takes a lot of work and confidence to go and get it. She sees her choices as attainable and matter-of-fact.

This is classic J. The other day at the grocery store the woman in line behind us asked J what she did (because the woman thought she looked familiar). Our hometown isn't exactly the size of Metropolis; it's Lincoln, Nebraska, where prominent citizens, like doctors, get recognized. J told the woman that she was an anesthesiologist at the hospital and the woman is like, "I always wanted to be a doctor." And so my wife goes, "Well, why didn't you?"

The woman had all these excuses, "Well, you know all that school and the cost and everything." And my wife, very matter-of-factly goes, "Look it's not rocket science. I got loans. I didn't have any money. I followed the path that was laid out for me. I had to work really hard, but it's all laid out for you on a path. If you want to be a lawyer or a doctor or a politician or whatever; you can go and do it. You put in the time, you follow the path and you get the payout."

People are always amazed that J went to sixteen years of school. She only hears that as a cop out—just another excuse. And seriously, she can't stand excuses. *It's too much time. It's too much money. It's too much work. I'm not smart enough.* She'd call you on it all. She'd say you either want it—or you don't. The rest is just the details—or excuses. When you sit down and talk to someone like that you get your shit in order. I know because I've seen it happen. She's always going out of her way, doing research and putting together life plans for practical strangers or finding specialists or new procedures for people who aren't even her patients. To me that's a whole lot more amazing than how much school she went to.

I have so much respect for my wife, but the way we each get to our goals is completely opposite. J will follow the path to the end of the day, putting in hours of work. For me, it's totally impossible to stay on the path. I'm working really fucking hard all the while, but I'm doing it while looking for angles and blurring the lines of that path—morally, ethically, and legally. That's just the way I'm wired. I can't stay on the path and I can't play by the rules. I will always find some way to get to the end quicker. Remember, I'm the second kind of person.

Even though we have opposite ways, we are constantly learning from one another. For example, I first got the value of my time thing from J. Suddenly I started to look at my choices differently. If I spend all day chatting online, what am I really accomplishing? If I spend all night online playing *Farmville* or *World or Warcraft*, what am I giving up? We go about our work in really different ways, but now I understand, like she always has, that time is everyone's most valuable asset. I don't waste it. (Which is why, honey, I paid sticker price for the BMW. ☺)

My wife proves every day that she has the chops to back up her opinions and I listen to her when she talks, even if I don't agree with her. At specific moments, listening to J was the smartest thing I ever did, like back when I was on unemployment looking for another day job. She told me not to get another job. She told me to invest my time fully into building my own thing. But that seemed impossible to me. Even though I had this really deeply-seated life perspective of fuck-everyone-I'm-going-to-do-it-my-way, you can't underestimate the lasting impact of negative reinforcement. Even as a married man in my thirties who was no longer fat, I still had the fat-boy mentality. I had been told I was a loser for so many years that my confidence was in the garbage. It still bothered me that I was voted most likely to end up on welfare. I still believed it when people told me that I'd never be anything without a four year degree. Negative reinforcement is a bitch that takes a really long time to break.

But I trusted J and she seemed to think that I was a no-brainer. You know what I mean, not that I didn't have a brain, retard. J saw that I had a unique ability and that I had proven over and over again that I could build these online properties and programs that people loved and used like crazy. For her it didn't make any sense for my successes to be one-offs that happened while I was trying not to get fired from another menial day job. She argued that if I focused full-time on doing my own thing instead of an hour here and there at night or secretly during the day, then I would find my success.

When she put it that way, suddenly my own path suddenly looked so obvious and simple. My deeply buried egotism and that sense of fuck-everyone-I'm-going-to-do-it-my-way started to grow into real, grown-up confidence. I started to believe what I know now—that I have no equal. I believed it and that was the key for me to go out and prove it time and time again. Today, when I participate in the largest Internet launches in the world I dominate with half the resources because I see angles and I'm willing to do what others are willing not to do. I dominate because that's how I'm wired. That's just the kind of guy I am.

It took J to cheerlead for me, though, and to do the bookkeeping and finances. It took her forcing me to sit down with my checkbook and learn how to budget, and save, and project, and not bounce four checks a month. It's still a pain in the ass. I hate that part, but I suppose it comes with this whole adult thing and I am willing to do my part in this amazing marriage I have going. I don't care who you are and how brilliant you think you are, you can't underestimate the value of marrying the right woman.

This was just around the same time that I got the Google call, which turned out pretty well for us, and only drove J's point home more convincingly. I think it's accurate to mark that time as my official launch into ShoeMoney land.

I'm a really good story-teller because I just have a knack for spinning things. My friends are always all, "Shoe, tell the one about roof golf again." I'm always cracking my wife up with some random story about something that happened during my day. And as a dad, it's one of the things I do best—breakfast stories, after school stories, bedtime stories, Santa stories. They're all good. But I don't think that even I, in all my story-telling glory can do an adequate job of describing to you how I felt at this time in my life. Suddenly I seemed to have it figured out.

I felt like a freakin' wild animal finally released from his cage. The cage was my obesity, bankruptcy, insecurity, loneliness—some crazy combination of all those things. And suddenly there I was—skinny, healthy, rich, successful and in love. I kind of went a little nuts, not crazy nuts—just really excited about everything. I started wearing so much gold jewelry that I put Mr. T to shame. I bought shit that drove my wife crazy—stuff I had always wanted but never could afford. I found a Movado Esperanza in a random jeweler's one day and bought it on the spot because the model was no longer in production and I had admired it for years when I was broke. I bought an H2 Hummer at sticker price off the lot one afternoon because I wanted to be that guy. I painted my toenails blue. I didn't care if I looked like a clown. I wanted to be the guy who lived as loudly as he possible could. It was fun.

Everything about that time was fun. My creativity was on the loose, too. NextPimp continued to kill it and I was bringing in obscene amounts of money through affiliate marketing. This whole experience opened up a brand new world to me. It was like a playground of ways to make money and that was infatuating.

I knew that the value of NextPimp would be nothing if the content wasn't awesome and the content would only continue to be awesome if my users were putting up a lot of it. I needed tens of thousands of uploads every day to stay progressive. Suddenly it occurred to me to incentivize my users by running contests. One month I gave away $500 to whoever uploaded the most ringtones. Another month the prize was a Corvette. This was simple, but it was one of the smartest things I did. It worked better than rocket science.

The other thing I knew was that people were stealing my shit, lifting content straight from my site as soon as it was up and transferring it to their own sites. I was never going to stop that, I knew. This was before YouTube and the DMCA and the whole area of copyright infringement was really gray. So I wasn't going to stop the stealing, but I thought I could defray it at least. I made a zip file so that when anyone downloaded a ringtone they actually downloaded a compressed file that included the ringtone and then another instructions folder (because people needed instructions on how to load their ringtones to their phone). The genius here was that within the instructions I led them back to the NextPimp site on a landing page that said, "This file was from NextPimp.com. If you'd like to donate for this service click here." On that page, I had a PayPal button set up so in one click they could donate what they wanted. Sure enough, people were readily donating $10 a pop. I actually started making a significant amount of money on donations and realized that there's psychology here. When you give someone something for free, they want to pay you back for that value. When they feel that it's voluntary, they're much happier to pay me than if I demanded a $10 membership fee.

I had three significant revenue streams going all at once. I had contextual ads (Google's AdSense product), I was an active affiliate marketer, and I was raking in donations. Things were good.

Side Note: I realize that a lot of you might not know anything about the world of affiliate marketing. It's not a complicated thing. Basically, as an Internet marketer you drive online traffic to specific sites and those sites pay you for getting people there. That's really all you need to know because the space of affiliate marketing as I knew it is now dead. Oh and also, it's not a good time to become an affiliate marketer. You should know that, too. And if you are an Internet marketer maybe this is a good time to start thinking about branching out to something new. Come, on and use your imagination or at least read my blog and rip off some of my newer ideas.

So everything was going awesome and J started talking about having a baby. I was like, "*Sure. Why not?! How hard could that be?!*" To be perfectly honest with you, I didn't give it a whole lot of thought after that. Remember, I never thought I would have a family so there weren't any worries pre-programmed into my head. In an interview not long ago the topic of family came up and this chick asked, "Would you say you were a natural father figure?" I laughed and was like, "No. I was naturally a jerk." I was an overly protective older brother. That was the closest I ever came to practicing my parenting skills before having kids.

Anyhow, (after a little bit of work ;)…) we got pregnant and before I knew it, out came my daughter, Juliet.

I have heard so many people say that the day of their kid's birth was the happiest day of their lives AND I CALL BULLSHIT ON THAT. It's not happy—it's scary as shit. I was scared out of my mind. Out of nowhere there's this new human being that is breathing and crying and looking to me to keep it safe. I remember looking at J and thinking, "*What the hell did we do?*" just as she was handing me the baby to hold. I told myself, "*It's cool. I'm good.*" In actuality, I was crapping in my pants and SCARED OUT OF MY FUCKING MIND.

Having a kid is scary. Now add that to a dad who has done zero preparation. Okay, that's not exactly true. I had done exactly one thing. I hired a nanny. And the only reason I even did that was because my wife happened to mention, offhand during a birthing class two weeks before Juliet's birth, that I worked at home and would now be a stay-at-home dad. As soon as I heard that I was like, "Wait…what? Uh…Hell no." Two days later, the nanny was hired.

Eventually the baby shock wore off and I got over myself. It turned out that babies are actually pretty easy. All they do is cry, eat and crap... a lot. You hold them and you coo a little bit and then they sleep...and sleep... and sleep some more. In retrospect, all of that is easy. Once they go mobile, that's when you're really in trouble. Then they start to talk, the drama begins and you basically kiss sleep goodbye forever. That is a forever that seems very real to me. I'm convinced that I will never sleep again. But it's worth it. I've done a lot of things in my life, great and crazy a like, but parenting is at the top. It's the best. It's also the craziest and the hardest.

Having a kid also means you can't work out of your basement anymore. You need to get an office. So I did, like a real grown up with a job to go to and a company to run. And since I was so grown-up and parental suddenly, we decided that was a good time to throw another one into the mix (baby, not a company, LOL).

And out came Joslyn, The Crazy. The Honey Badger. She's also known at The Trucker because she'll eat anything and craps like—well I'll leave that part out so she won't be totally furious with me in ten years. Actually, the Honey Badger doesn't give a shit.

Up to that point, Juliet's birth was the scariest moment of my life. That was because I didn't know what scary really meant yet. You don't know real fear until you know what it feels like to watch your child dying.

When Joslyn was born the doctors told us she had bacterial meningitis. They apologized with their eyes as they told us, very carefully, that she had a 10% chance of survival. If she did, somehow miraculously survive, they told us that she would be deaf and severely mentally retarded. We didn't even have time for this to sink in before they took her off to Omaha Children's Medical Center. She was on a feeding tube for the next few days. My wife sat next to her crib in the neonatal intensive care unit, day and night, watching her respirations and ready to intubate her own child should Joslyn stop breathing.

I'm not a crier. Maybe it's my meds. Maybe it's because I'm cold and detached. Maybe that's in my genes. It's just not me. Before Joslyn's birth the ONLY TIME I cried was when my grandpa died. When I held Joslyn's little body in my arms, all hooked up to a bunch of tubes, I bawled like a baby. When I think back it feels like I cried for a full two days. I couldn't function. J and I both got into separate car accidents during those two days because we had just shut off, I guess. The only thing I wanted to do was hold Joslyn and tell her stories. I told her about how her mom and I met. I told her how great her mom is and how she would see that and grow up with that. *Your mom is incredible. You will be incredible, too.* I told her how cool I could be and that once when J had my Astrovan it stalled out on the side of the road. I rolled onto the scene with a 2 liter of coke. I popped opened the hood, poured it over the battery and started the car. I came to the rescue, I told her. *Your dad is cooler than MacGuyver. I know you don't know who MacGuyver is, but trust me. He's pretty cool.* And then came the waterworks.

It was impossible that this baby was going to survive. And at the same time, it was impossible that she wouldn't.

Four days after she was born, a doctor walked into Joslyn's hospital room and was like, "Never mind."

Out of the blue, she started responding to the medication. That meant her case was actually viral, which is not nearly as serious. No one had an explanation. Mostly we got shrugs from the doctors. One said, "Something changed." And that was all.

It didn't make any sense. It was the same chart and the same tests and everything. Three different specialists had reviewed the information in addition to my doctor wife and all four of them agreed that Joslyn's was a case of bacterial meningitis. And then—it wasn't. Suddenly they told us she was going to be perfectly fine just because—well, she just was. It took me at least two weeks before I started to believe that Joslyn was going to be just fine. Today she is more than fine. She's The Honey Badger.

I spoil my kids. I buy them pretty much everything—pools and swing sets and the Barbie edition 4WD motorized Escalade and remote control helicopters and dolls and books and bikes. I buy them this stuff because I can and because I want them to have fun. A lot of it I do selfishly, because it's fun for me, too. The Escalade is a good example. It sat in the garage for a few years before either of the girls was old enough to cruise around the sidewalks. I just liked having it there, looking at it and imagining the Power Wheels fun I knew they would have in that thing.

I haven't exactly thought the whole thing through as a parenting philosophy. I don't think it will make a difference, though. I spoil my kids. So what?! J doesn't agree with me. She is very concerned about how there are going to "turn out." In response, I'm in the process of formalizing a fool proof parenting system. Maybe you can tell me what you think.

Here's what I've got so far:

The ShoeMoney 6 Step System for Raising Kick-Ass Kids
(Copyright pending)

1. Enforce chores immediately (before your kids realize they are spoiled Americans with "inalienable rights").
2. Start each day screaming 50 times in unison "I am a badass!"
3. Give your kids opportunities to practice being a badass.
4. Accept that your kids are, in fact, related to you and will take after you in lots of ways.

5. Know that you can't control everything.
6. Hire a nanny.

Here's what I mean.

Instilling a work ethic is one of the most important things all parents can do for their kids. I buy my kids all kinds of crap but most of it is really stuff that I want to have for us to play with together. The stuff that they really want, they work for. We have chore sheets that they are responsible for completing each week and my girls understand that these chores are their family responsibilities and are non-negotiable. They take pride in contributing in this way and really embrace their jobs. Now, I'm not talking about having the four year old dig out the driveway after a blizzard or anything. Their jobs are things like feeding the dog, bringing bedtime drinks to everyone's bedside, and overseeing all tooth-brushing activity. Every day the girls complete their chores they get closer to their paydays at the end of the week. At six and four, they already understand that you earn by working. But they also understand that earning isn't just about money. Some weeks they are motivated by the privilege of getting pierced ears or spending a special day with Mom. The point is that we take work ethic seriously. One thing that really bugs me is people who think they are entitled to things, just because. My girls will never be like that.

I had this one friend growing up. He was the laziest guy on the planet and he learned it from his parents. My dad always said his dad was the laziest guy he had ever met. For as long as I knew him his dad was on disability for a "neck injury." Fast forward a bunch of years and that kid went on to marry my sister's good friend. I was paying attention because I actually had a pretty good-sized crush on that chick all throughout the time she was dating Lazy Jr. But I was a 400 pound geek and he was a panty-dropper who spent money on chicks like it was water. Anyway, today those two are married and they have fully embraced his family's ways and "work ethic." I know for a fact that today Lazy Jr. is on disability for some "injury" and they get a ton of money from the government for their kids. Those next juniors are so fucked—for at least the third generation, if not the fourth and fifth and probably the sixth.

Side Note: Dude—you know who you are and if you are reading this I want you to know that you could make a fortune writing a book entitled, *How I Got through Life Living Off of You, The Working Suckers*. You really are a master.

Humility has its place in life. I DO KNOW that. But I'm more concerned with my kids having a strong sense of self-confidence. It's not that I want them to think that they're better than everyone else, but I also kind of do. Maybe this is because I spent so many years surrounded by negative reinforcement and a lot of self-doubt. Maybe that's why I've swung to the other extreme. I honestly feel that a kid who believes she is strong and talented won't make stupid decisions later on. Growing up, all the kids that I knew who did stupid shit were trying to prove something. They were like, "Look how cool I am or how crazy I am!!" I know because that kid was me a lot of time. A kid who already knows that she is the shit isn't living her life trying to impress anyone else. I want my girls to know that from the very beginning, not to have to wait until they truly believe it sometime in their thirties. For a lot of people, that can be too late.

But hollow self-confidence can also be a problem. Just like they earn their toys, my girls earn the praises they get. Recently, Juliet had a bowling field trip with her class. Before it started she and I went together to practice. Of course it was great to spend that time together, but that wasn't the main reason. We went so that on the day of the field trip she knew she could do it on her own and she wasn't scared or nervous. She smoked everyone, not because her daddy taught her, but because she learned how to master something independently. It made me really proud to watch her succeed like that and to hear her stories when she came home all pumped.

194

I have to tell you the potholder story. Now, remember that I'm crafty and I have a knack for finding angles. I'm willing to do things that others are willing not to do and all that. I write really awesome copy that convinces people to buy shit and have become an incredible marketer. That's me. And now I have these kids. So one day, when Juliet was four, it wasn't surprising when she came to me with this half-finished potholder and a plan. She wanted me to help her sell the thing on the Internet so that she could contribute money to one of the local soup kitchens I fundraise for.

I knew that I could just promote this thing to my list and we'd sell thousands, but we didn't have thousands—we only had one. Besides that, I wanted Juliet to experience the whole process. So we made a site at www.potholders.wordpress.com, uploaded a couple images that she took with her iPad, made a short "sales video" and a pasted in a PayPal button. Soup to nuts, we created the whole thing in thirty minutes. The video was hilarious. The site is still up if you want to see it. It was so funny; I thought it could go viral. Juliet, totally unscripted, was like, "Hi. I'm Juliet Schoemaker. I make potholders so we can make money to feed bums."

It was a great idea, with only one problem. In one day she sold several potholders. Now, Juliet had been working on making one for the better part of a week and it was still only a quarter of the way finished. J and I were both freaking out a little bit, sitting there staring dumbfounded at each other wondering how we got into this mess. That's when Juliet suggested that we just go to Target and buy a lot. She was absolutely right. We could buy them all day long from Target and still be able to deliver on her business model. The proceeds would still go straight to the goal—donations for the soup kitchen. That's my kid. Somehow she already understands scalability and sales structures.

Juliet's crafty like me and she's always ready to make a deal. Am I going to be angry or embarrassed that she didn't learn economics the Sesame Street way? Absolutely not. That kid is going to be a force to be reckoned with, because it's in her genes. That's just who she is. I'm not surprised when I see it. My kids are badasses after all.

And finally, when it comes to parenting, you have to remember that this whole thing is pretty random. Growing up, I had tons of different friends, from different walks of life. Of course there were the extreme examples, like Keith, but there were a lot of other stories and the one consistency that I can find between all of us and how we turned out is that sometimes it is just random. There was the one kid whose parents were total partiers and never supervised anything. But somewhere along the line they taught him something about finance. Even though we always had these totally insane parties at his house, somehow he turned out to be a completely normal and healthy guy who's great at finance. There was also the kid who came from a *Leave It to Beaver* type of household where everyone was perfect and lovely. And somewhere along the line that really fucked him up because he turned out to be a major meth-head who has been in and out of rehab facilities across the country.

As a parent, you start to think that every single thing you do for your kids, to your kids, or in front of your kids will stick on them and shape the person that they're becoming. But I'm realizing that it's not that simple. Sometimes the kid from the fucked up house turns out perfectly fine when the kid from the perfect house ends up really fucked. I'm doing everything within my power to give my girls the best childhood I know how to give. Outside of that, I'm just hoping for the best.

Oh, and if you really want to be a happy and healthy parent, please hire a nanny. That way you will get some sleep along the way and still have the time and energy to have sex with your wife every once in a while.

16
You May Address Me as Doctor Schoemaker

In this business, by the time you realize you're in trouble, it's too late to save yourself. Unless you're running scared all the time, you're gone.

-BILL GATES

Doctor Schoemaker or Doctor ShoeMoney. They're both fine. Professor Schoemaker is good too, especially if you have a question. ShoeMoney, Schoemaker. Doctor. Professor. Whatever you're more comfortable with is cool with me. It's not that I'm knocking titles and names here. My wife's a doctor, don't forget. I know, *almost* firsthand, how much time you have to invest to earn these titles. And I know how many hundreds of thousands of dollars they cost. So believe me when I say I'm not crapping on the value of an MD or PhD.

I'm really jealous actually.

Because when you say, "Hi I'm Doctor Whatever," what you're actually saying in the politest way possible is, "Shut the hell up and listen. I'm a whole lot more important than you."

This really hit me a few years ago when J and I went to Chicago and stayed at the Ritz for a little fifth anniversary celebration. She made a call down to housekeeping for extra pillows and was like, "Hi this is Doctor Schoemaker in room 1217. I need four pillows sent up right away. Two cotton and two feather. Thanks!" That's all she said and she walked into the bathroom. Now, if I had made the same call, I'm positive they would have thought I was a complete jerk. But not her, because she's a doctor. She can ask for anything she likes. She's that cool. I thought to myself, "*Why not me? Seriously?*" When J came back from the bathroom I told her, "Fuck it. I'm going to be the second Doctor Schoemaker in the family."

SERIOUSLY, WHY NOT?!

Well, J didn't think it was such a great idea. Not that there was any issue with me investing the time and money into a doctoral degree, since she knew I wasn't going to invest the time and money to go back to school to earn a degree the old fashioned way. Why take the long road, retards, when there is an honorary shortcut? That's just common sense, to me. But J was all bent out of shape and adamant that she wouldn't stand for it.

First of all, she didn't think that anyone in their right mind would confer any such thing. And I was like, "Honey, have you met the Internet?!" I knew I could find someone online to get me an official piece of paper, making me Doctor Schoemaker. And trust me, I knew exactly where I was going to hang it once I had it framed (next to all my other cool shit). But still that wasn't J's point. Sure, whatever, I'm a well-connected dude who could get an honorary degree, no problem. Her point was that it wouldn't mean anything once I had it in my hand. She wanted me to agree that I'd never have anyone address me as Doctor Schoemaker, because I hadn't earned it like she had, technically.

Technically, shnechnically.

I'm not a liar or a con artist who's trying to pull one over on you, here. I just don't think things like degrees or awards have this holy value in them that needs to be respected. I think everyone uses this stuff to get a foot in the door. Once you're there, you gotta' work, but getting in the door or getting publicity—well that's all a shit show where anything goes in my opinion. And if I need to use my title of doctor to get the good pillows delivered to my hotel room, you'd better believe I'm pulling out that card.

You have to leverage the opportunities at hand. I'm not just talking about good pillows and doctorate degrees here. My business is almost all Internet based and the key to being a successful Internet marketer is being able to get people's attention. OMG I can't even begin to tell you how valuable the pictures I have collected have proved to be. Obviously there was the AdSense check from Google in 2005. I asked J to take that picture of me holding the check. She didn't understand why and made me promise not to show anyone. Sorry babe. I broke one :(. But that image has gotten me so much traffic, it's sick.

In 2004, my wife and I were leaving our hotel room at the Bellagio when all of a sudden Paris Hilton walked around the corner. I pumped up the nerve and asked if I could get a photo with her. My wife was all rolling her eyes and interrupted us like, "Oh, honey…please. She is busy. Leave her alone." I stared at her with a death look until she got the camera out. I got the photo and have leveraged that every which way you can imagine (except for insinuating that I was a part of her sex tape collection, but maybe that's not such a bad idea…).

In 2007, I was at the Tech Crunch Awards and pissed next to Zuckerberg. I know what people say about him, but he was pretty cool and all, considering I asked him to pose for a picture as we left the bathroom. I got that one too. It hangs on the wall of fame in my office with the tons of other people I have met. The list goes on and on with celebrities and stuff. I travel a lot. I speak a lot. I meet a lot of famous people. They really aren't hard to find. I'm guessing you have had some of these opportunities too. The difference is that most people (yes, probably you) think they're too cool to look star struck and badger someone famous for a photo. Well, good for cool little you. You're sitting home with a bare wall while I leverage all these photos to the hilt.

I guess what I mean to say is that those thirty seconds of awkwardness can pay dividends for life. Stop trying to be so cool, already, and focus on what you can leverage.

Now back to the doctor thing. I was pretty sure I could get an honorary doctorate and I knew I could leverage that some way too. The question in my house was-could I actually use it as my title?

I put it out to a poll on my blog and the masses responded. I bet you can guess the results.

Every doctor said that if I was given an honorary doctorate I could definitely NOT USE the title.

Every non-doctor said that if I was given an honorary doctorate I should definitely USE the title at my pleasure.

Now I'm reconsidering something I said earlier. Maybe there are actually three types of people in the world. There are those who want to follow a path and the rules along the way (the doctors). There are those who don't want to follow a path and the rules along the way if it takes too much effort (the non-doctors). And there are those who are crazy enough to blaze a completely new path with rules that are made up along the way and broken just as quickly (the honorary Doctor Schoemakers).

Because in my mind, a piece of paper at the end of a crap load of classes doesn't mean any more than a piece of paper at the end of a crap load of life experience. I'm like the soldier, not the student and in the battlegrounds of Internet marketing I have got plenty of field experience. In my area, I have earned a doctorate with scared piss and bleeding wounds and hundreds of thousands of my own dollars that were invested without the promise of a valuable piece of paper and a nice, cushy job.

There are some things in life that you just can't learn in a classroom— like the wild west of the online world. This space just moves too fast to study and enact. By the time something's trendy it's already "trended" across the Internet. By the time something is safe and sure, it's surely not going to be lucrative. If you want to make money online you have to be crafty. You have to be willing to take risks and be a little piss in your pants scared because you've just floated $10k on a hunch when you only have $2k to your name. You have to be willing to bend the lines morally, legally and ethically. I've said it before and I'll say it again:

You have to be willing to do what others are willing not to do.

A few years ago the University of Nebraska invited me to give a guest lecture to their school of business and the kids who were studying Internet marketing. Specifically, they asked me to lecture on the topic of Search Engine Optimization (SEO). Now, I didn't want to be a dick by telling all those kids that they were wasting their time, but I also didn't want to be a boring white dude spewing off numbers and formulas that I knew would never get them anywhere in the real world. I didn't want to waste anyone's time so when I stood up in front of those kids the first thing I said was, "SEO is bullshit."

When they didn't pull my plug right away, I kept going, explaining that SEO is very, very simple. And then I said that they had probably been taught what worked in SEO four years ago. I wasn't trying to piss anyone off, honestly, or to get anyone to drop out, but what I wanted them to realize was that if they were not working on this kind of stuff at home all the time, then they were wasting their time. And when they did get out of school, whatever kind of grades they pulled out wouldn't matter. They might get jobs, but studying Internet marketing from a book would never teach them anything that was progressive and significant. The electronic world just moves too fast for traditional school to make sense.

Let's just say, I got their attention.

A hundred hands shot up and of course the first question was, "So what do you do then? What would you tell me to do tomorrow to make money online?" That comment came from this little brunette.

I was like, "Why wait until tomorrow?" And then I brought her up to the stage.

This was all great theatrics, and at the time, I was pretty damn proud of myself for completely capturing the attention of the room. But as that chick was walking onto the stage I got a little nervous because I was completely flying impromptu and I had no idea if anything I was going to try would actually work. But here she was on the stage and I had to do something.

Thinking on my feet, all I could come up with was something I might do when I was sitting on my ass and screwing around online at home, late at night. I pulled up a site called Commission Junction on the LCD so the room could see it. Then I had this chick log into my account. We pulled up a random two page insurance offer and she read the specifics. The affiliate deal said we would earn $5 for every insurance quote that was filled out from the traffic we drove there. We grabbed the affiliate link and went into a forum on Craigslist. I had her write a little copy saying something like, "Hey guys. I don't know if this is real or not. Does anyone have any experience with this website? I filled it out and it said I was going to save a lot of money but I don't know if it's a scam…" And then she pasted the link.

The brunette sat down and I went on with my talk.

About ten minutes later as I'm ripping apart their latest reading assignment another hand shoots up and this kid goes, "I wonder if we made any money yet."

I'm thinking there's a ten to one shot that we haven't made a cent yet, but I had to reward this kid who at least had his mind on the prize. A little reluctantly, I logged back into my account and—sure as shit after bran—we had made fifteen bucks. In ten minutes (for about two minutes of creative thinking) we had driven three different people to fill out the insurance quote and earned fifteen bucks to boot.

The professor was in the front row rolling his eyes. Then I decided to add on a little public service announcement. I was like, "Now listen everybody, what we just did is called spam. But if you need to do this to learn how affiliate marketing works then I don't have a problem with it. But I can tell you that Craigslist would have a problem with it if you were trying to make a living just doing this."

So I covered my ass, but the point I left them with, at least, was that in this business it's all about getting people's attention. It is about finding angles that create interest and bringing in traffic. And you can't learn that in a book or a classroom even if you have the top five professors in the country following you around for twelve years, feeding you ideas and wiping your ass.

You've come all this way with me, and you've read on in good faith, supposing that I know something about something that I can teach you after all of this. But I'm not sure that that's the case. I mean, I know a lot about a lot. Through all my escapades I have learned at least a dump truck full of truths about life and business. The thing is that you have to learn many of these lessons for yourself, by going through your life while taking risks and choosing the adventure that takes you off the path. You have to be, as I've said, scared shitless a lot of the time to really reach your potential.

If one thing can translate off the page and into your life it might be this: You will have times in your life—everyone does—when opportunities present themselves. They come and then they go. They never last. And it usually feels scary when they come, because it's something new and unchartered. The question for you is: Are you going to seize your opportunities? Are you going to differentiate yourself and take risks? I give myself a lot of credit for being able to find these opportunities and (as you have noticed) I like to call them angles. But the real fact is that everyone sees angles. Just very few have the balls to exploit them.

I have the balls. I can whip out a list of accomplishments to prove it.

From 2003 – 2009 I built that little property called NextPimp, which I have already told you a lot about. But the list has to start here because this was the time when I realized that I was my own best day job—that my ideas were worth every second of the time I spent to build them out. That was the first NextPimp lesson.

Over the years one of my mantras has also become, "Build websites for people, not for search engines." That also started with NextPimp. I created it first to help me pimp out my own personal Nextel while I realized that hundreds of thousands of other people would use it too. It was a great free service for people to upload and subsequently share the ringtones they created. At its peak the site had 135,000 unique visitors per day, and not because I was tricking anyone into going there, but because it was a valuable service. At the end of the day, if you build a quality property, the money will come just as it did with NextPimp (which eventually generated **daily revenue between $10,000 and $14,000**).

Although NextPimp's revenue came mostly from Google's AdSense product I also learned that affiliate networks and donations were extremely profitable and in the process I remembered an old lesson about story telling. If you remember, back in the day I pulled off a really ballsy insurance scam, which worked specifically because of the credibility of the source. No one was going to question two pillars of the community when they reported a case of car vandalism in the middle of the night. They were the right storytellers for the police audience and my little scam worked. NextPimp was never a scam, but it occurred to me somewhere along the line that most of my users were not Midwestern white boys. Most of the people pimping out their Nextel phones were young black Americans. So as the owner of the site I became Mike Lowery, borrowing the name from *Bad Boys*, and inheriting a reputation as this nice dude who was helping the brothers out. It wasn't a coincidence that once this alias was public, my donation revenues took off.

I sold the property in 2009 because I lost interest in the quality of the site and I have learned that once that happens, the value will never rebound. That is the time to take a payday and move on to what thrills you.

At that time what was most thrilling to me (as always) was finding new ways to make a buck (or twenty thousand). I realized in my time touring around as a speaker for Google, that this was a unique talent. People starting asking me who I was writing for. So in 2003, I started my own blog at Shoemoney.com. Nine years later, ShoeMoney.com reaches over 200,000 people daily. It has been listed in Technorati's top 50 most read blogs on the Internet and #1 in Internet marketing since 2005. It also is consistently ranked in the top 5 marketing blogs in the world on the prestigious Adage Power 150 Internet Marketers. It was also in Business Week as the top 5 money making blogs on the Internet. It's often classified as a blog for Internet Marketers, Marketing Strategies, SEO, and Making Money Online.

But the truth about my blog is that I started it as a personal blog—a place to chronicle my different ideas and experiences in real time as I was experimenting and learning about the art of money making. It was also the perfect place to catalog the pictures I was collecting at the different conferences I attended. When I first started, I wrote 1.5 posts a day. The posts were mostly about how I was building, marketing and monetizing NextPimp. And absolutely no one read. I got used to that say-whatever-the-hell-I-want kind of stage where I could promote what I liked and slam all the dickheads I met along the way. Then I published my legendary Google check in 2006 and everything went viral.

Images are often the catalyst for a tidal shift in popularity. A picture is worth a thousand words. That's truth. But to keep a crowd, you have to have the words to back up any picture—even if it has a million links.

The blog continues to grow year over year and in 2012 it will make an estimated $1.5 million from advertising, selling my own products, and promoting other people's products. I have to think this is because I have never sold out my words. I write it myself, with my own messy grammar and honest ideas. People go to Shomeoney.com to get ShoeMoney and that's what they will always get—crass, unfiltered, unapologetic and well…right. LOL ;)

In 2007, I built a property called Auction Ads. It was a display advertising network powered by eBay. eBay has an affiliate program that pays out compensation both for new account referrals and click-through purchases. Auction Ads was simply an advertising network which enabled affiliates to automatically and continuously query eBay for products that matched their content and user interests. These products would automatically be displayed on the affiliate's site along with the price and remaining sale time. Affiliates were paid each time a user clicked on an ad and took action. I came up with the idea because, again, I was lazy. I didn't want to have to do manual searches for products, I just wanted it automated, because—you know, that's me.

But this idea wasn't exactly revolutionary. When I launched the company on March 4th there were seven other sites, which did nearly the exact same thing as Auction Ads. But I saw an angle and was willing to do things that my competitors were willing not to do. eBay pays out all of its affiliates and affiliate networks in 60 day terms, which means that it could take 60 full days before you see a dime from the eBay purchases your site traffic drives. They do this to ensure there is enough time to review activity and transactions and also to mitigate the risk of fraudulent activity. I wrote a program to instantly sniff out the cookie stuffers and cheaters on Auction Ads so I wasn't facing any fraudulent risk. I realized that my angle in the market would be the quick payout and I decided to pay my publishers out on what is called Net Zero Terms.

This was great for my publishers and the only downside for my value was that I was always floating the money. I didn't start the company with any capital, so within four months what I was earning and owed monthly from eBay was already paid out to my publishers, at peak in the sum of $2 million. The site was completely cash poor, and my money was nothing more than constantly shifting numbers in accounts. On paper, however, it was ridiculously attractive as a component property because it had all the traffic. Most importantly, because I never had a capital investment and had taken all the risk personally, the entirety of Auction Ads was mine. That is until I sold it to a large NYC based advertising company when it was four and a half months old.

My lawyers tell me I can't disclose the sale price, but I can say it made me very happy. (Ear to ear, baby.) The sale also made my programmer, David Dellanave, an instant millionaire. He worked for me for four months and I paid him twenty bucks an hour. Everyone thought I was crazy when I made the seven figure wire to him but I thought it was the right thing to do. I would do the exact same thing today because the site's value had everything to do with the work we invested together, which included many sleepless nights in a row. And to me, that's worth something. Seven figures of something, at least.

After the Auction Ads sale I had so much momentum and clout that I was a major force. That was the time when Business Week contacted me to ask how the hell I was ranked fifth on their list of biggest money making blogs. They hadn't really heard of me yet, and I was ranked just under the Huffington Post. That's when you're the hottest, when people think you've appeared magically, as if out of nowhere—an overnight millionaire success. Almost immediately, I had people flying into Lincoln, paying $25K to sit in my offices and spend two hours with me. That was nice, I guess.

But the thing you never forget—which is never tiring to talk about—is the moment when you personally know you've made it. For me, it was the first time I was invited by Tech Crunch, the biggest technology website in the world, as a part of the press team to cover their annual awards show. That event is no joke. It's the most prestigious awards forum that exists and for me, to be there and offer my ideas and opinions of the newest innovations, well that was nothing short of surreal. I was in the press pit next to the reporters from Forbes and Wall Street Journal and stood up and waved after being introduced as the #1 Financial Blogger in the world, since at the time the category "Internet Marketing" didn't even exist.

You don't sit on the moment when you're interviewing Mark Zuckerberg and Kevin Rose and the founders of MySpace and Digg. You leverage it. You make friends and you make sure you're always so damn relevant you're ranked in the Top 100 most read blogs in the world.

Because I have built up all this experience in Internet marketing— blazing the path before it even existed in name—I can go into any company and do the best thing that I do: strategize. As a consultant, every company is a new idea for me and a new expansion in the "How can I increase the revenue?" game. I study everything they're doing— infrastructure, security, affiliate marketing, donations, subscriptions, products, SEO services—and put it back together the way it will work best in each case.

It's no secret that the most successful Internet marketers of yore are now the highest paid consultants for two reasons. First, it's still cheaper to employ my services as a consultant than to build it up themselves. The payroll and resources would never figure out. But more importantly, no agencies have the hands-on know how. The marketing agencies are doing the same thing that the kids in the lecture halls are doing and studying how things work will never be the same as actually doing it.

Because I'm experimenting and leveraging and learning and blogging, I'm constantly ahead of the curve in knowing how to dominate the market. That's my brand. That's what ShoeMoney is all about.

In 2008, I saw that there was a call for a package of Internet marketing tools. I bundled together everything I was using in-house for SEO and Pay-Per-Click advertising and called it ShoeMoney Tools. In the first month it was available we did over $60,000 in revenue. We still run it with updates because it's valuable and relevant and therefore it continues to be a great stream of revenue.

For some reason 2009 was the year of the "guru," during which a handful of hacks came out with magic pill versions of money making Internet programs. Not surprisingly, 99% of them were junk. Mostly to expose the crap value that these idiots were producing, I hired a video team of my own and created The ShoeMoney System. I produced my "how-to" as a 9 module system in which I took an average local recording artist and walked her through monetizing her own site and content online. The videos were all recorded live with no stunt antics or fancy formatting. It's just plain old good information. To date we have done over $10 million in gross sales of that product.

Side Note: I hate the term guru. Even if we're in the Himalayas or some shit I don't want to hear anyone use that term. And guess what, if someone calls themselves a guru I can guarantee you 100% that they're completely full of it. Don't listen or buy a thing from them. Consider yourself warned.

There is a lot of SEO snake oil out there, always has been. Part of it has to do with the term, I think. It sounds so misleadingly technical. *Search Engine Optimization.* When actually the trickiest thing about SEO is that there is no real way to quantify whatever optimization you achieve. Google changes its algorithms constantly without reporting what kind of results your specific methods get, while the only guidelines they ever report are too basic to give you any relevant feedback. In 2011, I got to thinking what bullshit this was and decided to share the same programs that I built and used for SEO on my own sites. I called it Free SEO Report.

In a lot of ways the evolution of Free SEO Report was really similar to NextPimp. I wrote a program that I used daily; I found a lot of value in it and figured that other people would, too. On the site all you had to do was to enter your domain, the keyword for which you wanted to improve your search engine ranking and an email address where the report could be sent. The report would show not only where you were ranked at that moment, but also show you a comparison of your optimization method alongside the methods being used by the current top ten ranked results in Google. Via our reports you not only learned the rank results, but were exposed to the "magical" doings of your competition.

The value from a single report was amazing. But I knew the real value for any SEO-er would be in having access to unlimited reports. In the time since building NextPimp, I had also learned a huge amount in regards to purchasing psychology and price points. For example, I learned that everyone likes a $19.95 price so much that—nine times out of ten—your buyer is more likely to click and pay $19.95 for three months (or one month!) as opposed to $25 per year. I applied what I learned regarding pricing to this project. At Free SEO Report you were given your first report free. After that you could buy individual reports for $10 a piece or you could do a monthly subscription at $19.95 and receive unlimited reports. That worked beautifully and was in my opinion, a uniquely valuable service.

The biggest mistake you can ever make with a successful online property is to neglect growth. At the end of the day the value of every site is its traffic and when you have five bites you have to be thinking about turning that into twenty. That's where the beauty of referrals comes in. Once I introduced the referral program on Free SEO Report, which awarded an additional free report for each new referral, the site spread like wildfire. Before I blinked again we had between 400 and 600 users daily. That's a shit ton of daily traffic for such a niche service.

After running the site for four months, the database reached 20,000 users and I decided it was ripe to sell. For me, the maintenance of the site wasn't worth the revenue that it was creating through such a moderately priced product. And I am not an SEO company. I knew that this site, which was capable of bringing in 600 new leads a day, would be extremely attractive to an SEO company so I started shopping it around. The moral of this story is twofold. First, I learned unequivocally, that sales is nothing but psychology and second, it sometimes pays off to spend all night watching an entire season of a television show.

I spent about a month soliciting SEO companies to buy my site, for a fairly negligible price. No one bit and I started to get a little pissed off. Then one day someone in the office mentioned the series *Shark Tank*, which features these entrepreneurs who come on the show with a service or product and work with these sharks to structure crazy ass deals with investors. I looked it up that night and was totally hooked. I stayed up the whole night and watched every episode of the first season. Randomly, the next day, while I was suffering from a no-sleep hang-over I got a call back from one of the SEO companies I had solicited a month before. They said they heard I was looking to "unload" Free SEO Report and they might be interested. Amped up by the sharks arrogance and ownership, I immediately responded in a tone that was completely different from all my previous sales conversations. Suddenly I wasn't looking to "unload" this thing I had built, I was possessive and protective and threw out all sorts of terms like retaining 10% ownership to be sure they wouldn't strip and scrap my baby and demanding 25% of any resale price they flipped it for. In a half an hour I had structured a deal to sell Free SEO Report for three times what I couldn't before. Let me say that again. **I negotiated a deal to sell something at three times the price I couldn't unload it for the week before.** SEO Link Wheelers ended up with enough daily leads to feel like they bought pure gold and I deposited a value that was forty times the monthly gross revenue.

I know that what I have is a gift. I'm not being an arrogant ass when I say that I have a talent for invention. It's just the truth. And this makes me well-suited for the ever-changing nature of the technological world. I have run and gunned my way through the woods and I'm almost always running scared because I'm running someplace new. Scared is just one word for it though, a dramatic way to say that if you don't know what you're doing, exactly, you're probably doing something right, or new at least.

These days I'm not running scared, I'm just aware. I'm aware that the affiliate space as I knew it is dead. I'm aware that my last crazy scheme is not behind me. I'm aware that tomorrow you can always find yourself bankrupt again and the day after that you could be on the cover of Forbes. I'm also aware that blazing new trails with the likes of Gates and Jobs and Trump often means that you leave your family behind and neglected. I'm mostly aware that I'm smart enough to find another way through where I can have a better quality of life with a company that sustains my inventiveness.

So my latest project is building out my brand into a real grown-up company that is around for the long haul, not an idea that floats along until it crashes or is bought up by someone else to run. But when you make such an immense shift, like completely changing your company's culture, you have to reassess the team. For me, it meant letting go of every employee because I had to start fresh. I knew it had to start just with me and a revolutionary idea. Everything else can be built up around me. That's just how I operate.

I brainstormed until I came up with my best new idea. I call it the PAR Program. PAR stands for *people acquisition and retention*. It's revolutionary because we're rewriting the online user experience to acculturate client relationships and retention. Essentially, we're pioneering the art of lasting client/server relationships within the instant gratification of a virtual world. The company is currently five months old and we are approaching our 40th client. It's so revolutionary we've got an old school waiting list in action until we can hire and train the right client managers.

Through everything I've experienced so far, I know it's always the right time for a revolutionary idea. If you can see the angle, the only questions is, "Are you ballsy enough to take it down?"

So you can call me whatever you like, but just so you know the fine people at Kazakhstan University thought me worthy of a doctorate. They sent it to me a few weeks after I posted the poll on my blog. I hung it inside my office, next to my pictures with Paris and Mark and MC Hammer and Joe Rogan and my features in Forbes and the Wall Street Journal and the New York Times and TechCruch and Fast Company.

It says:

Kazakhstan University

School of International Business

AWARDS

Jeremy "ShoeMoney" Schoemaker

THE

Doctorate of Internet Marketing

The letters are all fancy. I think they're calligraphy or something, but it's definitely official. And there's a bunch of Arabic-y letters in there, too. I don't know what they say. I don't care. It's a doctoral diploma; I have one and you can check it out if you stop by my offices the next time you're in Lincoln.

In your opinion, maybe that doesn't legitimately make me a doctor. But to tell you truth, I don't care. It's valuable to me and I'll leverage it any way I see fit. Maybe you just don't get it because the whole idea is revolutionary. Maybe that's the way people will really earn their degrees in the next century. At the end of nine years of real world curriculum a diploma will arrive from half way around the world and then everyone will have to address you as Doctor Whatever. You know what? I should really keep that one to myself.

Just remember you heard it here first and yes, you may address me as Doctor Schoemaker.

17

Holy Shit

Success is a lousy teacher. It seduces smart people into thinking they can't lose.

—BILL GATES

Maybe I should have written two books—one about my crazy life and one about my business philosophies. But I didn't. I don't know how to separate one from the other. That's just how I've always been. That's how my blog has always been, so I guess that's just how this book has always had to be, even before I decided to write it.

The problem with business specific books is that they really can't be specific. The only way to do your business the best possible way is to do it authentically. You know what I mean? Everything else can be ripped off and hacked and gimmicked. In that sense, there really is no sound business specific advice that I can give to you. And I refuse to be generic. So instead, I'm going broad and all in here in this almost final chapter.

First I want to talk about what I call my Coke Theory.

I actually learned this way back in the day, before I had any business at all, as I watched my dad building his two companies. If you remember, he started his first company, Admiral Improvement, because there was a need and he had an expertise. He saw an angle and took the opportunity to make a lot of money from Case by building streamlined replacement pieces for all its tractors. And once he had that facility, he used part of it to make a new product: the crippled alewife fishing lure.

I got nervous when he sent his prototypes out to the local fishermen for testing because I thought someone would steal this million dollar idea. But my dad explained to me that without a factory full of scrap metal and metal cutters and paint and paint machines it would cost an average guy a million dollars of investment before he ever saw penny of profit. And that's not exactly the kind of million dollar idea that people like. The initial investment is too big. But in my dad's case, he already had all the machinery he needed for the fishing lures. It didn't cost him anything extra to introduce a new product. (By the way: I think the lures could have been gravy if he had had the tenacity to keep going, but that's not my point. We're not headed back to stuff with my dad. I already ragged on him a lot and I know that he did the best job he could, so I'm letting that go.)

The point here is a business one. **Once you have started to build something, the smartest thing you can do is to keep going and use what you already have to make more and new and better.**

That's the Coke Theory basically. You see, if you're Coca-Cola, what you do is keep making Coke. And then you make Diet Coke and Cherry Coke and Vanilla Coke and Coke Zero. That's all great. It will all work great because you have the resources already in place to keep making Coke-related products. But if you wake up one day and decide it's time to make coffee, well that's a whole different story.

This lesson came early on and I never forgot that the smart thing is to build up the basic resources you need and then you keep going, drawing from them and investing back into them. But resources aren't just capital like money, factories and raw materials. It's more than that. I learned much later on that authority and audience are, sometimes, more important than everything else. And I learned this the hard way.

Once I realized that I was a brand, I did everything ShoeMoney. It was the ShoeMoney blog, the ShoeMoney System and ShoeMoney Tools. Also I have the Elite Retreat, which isn't stamped with my superhero logo, but it's basically all my stuff and my way of thinking packaged as a high-end conference. I have all these things in my "factory" and if one does well, they all benefit and keep getting bigger and better.

Perfect time for a tangent, since I have neglected to explain Elite Retreat to you.

In 2005, I was at a social media/SEO conference in Vegas called PubCon and I started talking shop with my friend, Lee Dodd. PubCon is good and all. It definitely has its value, but because it's so big, the value it holds for various attendees is vastly different.

Our big complaint at the time was that the main components of the conference—the content sessions—were not helpful to us. We were, after all, already friends with most of the speakers and we had heard all their craziest stories, which was a hell of a lot more than they would be giving out during an impersonal twenty minute stage presentation.

For us, the real value of attending any event was getting face-to-face time to talk to people and hear about real live stuff they were doing within the industry. And as time went by, I was quickly becoming THE GUY that other people were seeking out for face time. I love meeting new people, telling a wild story and inspiring them to go out and find their own success, but this was how I spent 95% of my time at big conferences. Out of the 1000 people I would meet, there were never more than ten who had something exciting to offer me. Out of those ten, at a really awesome conference, you might end up with—MAYBE—two new contacts that were actually honest, legit and up for some kind of collaboration.

Don't quote me on the math there; percentages and probabilities aren't my thing on paper like they are in a negotiation. What I do know, though, is how to make something work in real life. While we sat at that conference together, making fun of all the other lanyard wearers, Lou and I cooked up a new plan for a super-focused and value-crazy, off-the-charts conference.

The key was that the structure of this new conference wouldn't be the content sessions. Instead, the whole thing would be based and built around networking. We decided to make it high-priced and personalized. The first price tag was $5,000 per attendee and we had everyone fill out an application covering what they did (specifically), annual gross revenues, and most importantly the topics and speakers that were most interesting, urgent, and top-of-mind for them. Lastly, we agreed that we wanted more partners to collaborate in building this new type of event—people that were like us: influential, but sort of lonely and looking for adventurous partnerships.

Honestly, I don't remember who first threw out the name Elite Retreat, or who was first to pull the trigger and make it known this was going to happen, but it seems like something I would do. On that note, I'm going to say it was me for full credit. By the time we left the PubCon, *all thanks to me*, we were ready to build Elite Retreat.

I contacted Aaron Wall and David Taylor because those guys were our first choice for partners. Aaron Wall was, and still is, the leading expert in SEO. He literally wrote the book on it. It's called *SEO Book* and has sold approximately a bazillion copies. Dave was a blogging king. His site was the textbook example of blog monetization. Even though, at this time my blog had a readership of approximately next-to-zero, they took my calls, heard the idea and signed on.

As the four founders of Elite Retreat, we held our first event in San Antonio in 2005. The price tag remained as planned: $5,000 per attendee, which was 7-8 times more expensive than any other industry conference (again, be easy on my math). When the advertisements first went live, our idea was not well received. Tons of people wrote about what a sham it was going to be and how there was no chance any conference value would justify that type of cost.

Well, it sold out.

So did the second one.

Now, keep in mind that we were not conference producers. We had never done this before and didn't have the business model down. As a business, it wasn't profitable and therefore, not successful. But as an idea, it was wildly successful. Exactly as intended, everyone made new contacts, networked their brains out and left with a huge impact for their businesses (Lou, Aaron, David and me included).

Here was the rub. Because this was our baby, we spent thousands of hours planning and executing the first two conferences and thus, they were wildly successful. By the time we got to the third, we were overly confident and stretched too far. So we outsourced all the logistics and promotions to a third party. Since these people were experts in the business of conferences, we figured it would fly, if not as well as than better than any event four Internet dudes could string together. But because we weren't involved and obsessed with every detail of the third Elite Retreat (or maybe because it had been scheduled in Orlando), it was a disaster before it even happened. Nothing was done right—top to bottom—and a month before the event there were a measly ten registered attendees.

With that registration, if we had decided to hold the event, balls blazing, we would have lost at least $20,000. The whole experience was personally embarrassing. It felt like my brand got shit on by a huge ass horse putting down a load. But there was no choice. We had to cancel it. So we did.

As far as my three partners were concerned, Elite Retreat was dead and gone. They were all frustrated and so was I. We had egg on our faces. (Which would have to be raw egg, right? How else would it stick? Just saying...) Man, do people love to kick you when you're down. I honestly think that tons of people wanted to see us fail. Especially the haters who originally thought the whole thing was a sham. Needless to say, we got a lot of bad publicity and eventually everyone else bailed. Like I said, it was like a huge ass horse dropping a steaming load.

There is something inside of me that ticks to the beat of a song called, "I DON'T FUCKING FAIL." And this is all the time, especially when I'm down. So, with the blessing of my partners, I took over the Elite Retreat, determined that I would figure out how to revive it and keep it running as the most kick-ass event in our industry from year to year to year.

I wouldn't fail.

It wouldn't fail.

Not even close.

I had the idea, the vision and the confidence that it could work, but no real experience in this business. So I did what I do? I started talking. I talked to everyone I could find in the events industry and figured out what might seem obvious to anyone who knows how to run a conference.

And I will give you what I learned right here, at no extra cost above the price of this honey of a book. Behold the basics for holding a successful annual conference (just in case you might be able to use them):

- **Staff.** You must have a full-time, year round event director on staff. This person's one and only job is to produce a killer event.
- **Brand awareness**. I achieved this through different press opportunities over the course of the year. Because I was running it solo I could use my brand and my audience as the starting point for recognition. I propped the event up on my ShoeMoney shoulders, you could say. People don't want to go to just any conference. People want to go to the "right" conference. People associated me with being ballsy and wildly successful so the event took on that same tone. The more

people who caught onto that, the more demand I had and so on.

- **SPONSORS**. We had never gone after sponsors before. I thought it was cheap to have another company foot the bill. But I realized that I needed others to have skin in the game (not time and interest and connection, just the money part). Sponsors are the perfect partners in this way.

With those tweaks Elite Retreat began under the ShoeMoney reign.

I hired a young guy named Tigh Buckles, with experience in the business of running conferences—DUH. And he was awesome. We got a ton of positive press with intermittent press releases and random interviews, like one I did on an in-flight radio show. We got amazing sponsors because the pitch was simple. *"You spend $20,000 for a booth at a show, give away a bunch of plastic shit and branded pens, and never talk to single decision maker with any type of budget. Sponsor Elite Retreat and you'll have a captive room of 30 guys who call every shot."*

It wasn't rocket science.

One day, four months before the event, Tigh came into my office and told me not only were we sold out, but we were already profitable by $60K.

Here's the other thing, which you probably aren't going to believe. My plan had never been to profit much with this event. The most important idea was that Elite Retreat remained the best possible, badass, valuable event my industry knows. This was even more important now that the conference was an extension of my brand. So I took what we made on that event and decided to blow the tops off of everything.

Let's just say, I *ShoeMoneyed* it.

If I was going to make money with this event, I decided to pour it all right back in and produce the dream for my colleagues every year. Any time I had to make a decision I thought of it as if I was going to be an attendee. Let's use selecting restaurants as an example. I would be like, "What are the three hottest restaurants in Miami that I've always wanted to go to?" And that's where we'd have dinner.

Other changes we made included:

- We picked up every attendee from the airport in their own, personal limousine.
- We hosted a meet and mingle cocktail reception the night before the event officially started.
- We made a full bar available every day during sessions starting at 9 am because some people need that lubrication before they can come out of their shells and get the full benefit.
- We took everyone out for a 5 star dinner every night of the event.
- We took everyone out to the most prestigious night clubs in town each night during the event.
- I made EVERYONE sign a non-disclosure agreement, which made it illegal for anyone to discuss anything that they saw or heard at the event. It wasn't actually enforceable, but it worked beautifully as a marketing ploy to emphasize the exclusivity of the event.
- And just as icing on the cake, everyone got a new iPad.

That about broke us even and—holy shit, what an awesome event it was.

We kept the same model in place as we developed year after year, while continuing to improve what was already the best event in the industry. It's always about fun and value. I focus on the booze, the parties, interesting people and prolific speakers who are each all-stars in the marketing community like Tim Ferris, Gary Vaynerchuk, Guy Kawasaki, Michael Sprouse, and Seth Godin.

Like I told you earlier, I build websites for people, not search engines. I carried that mantra with me into the event space and then I pushed it even further. I built Elite Retreat—not just for people—I built it for myself, and filled it with people that are interesting to me. Hell, I will admit that some days I think I built the whole thing just to surround myself with the people, the few people, who really amaze me. And lo and behold, it worked. I built Elite Retreat for me and my colleagues, definitely not for the sponsors. But you know what? In a few years I got the biggest hitting sponsors in the industry: Facebook, Microsoft, Google, Go Daddy, and Host Gator. All of those guys came knocking. Honestly, these days you can gauge how serious a company is within the Internet marketing space by when and if they've ponied up the money to become an Elite Retreat sponsor.

If I can drive home anything here it's that quality products are only quality products if the people who make them are focused on THE PRODUCT. They not only want to make it good, they want to continue making it better. But this kind of passionate dedication takes time. Too often people are seduced by the promise of a payoff in a microwave second. Get in that game if it tempts you. Go ahead and make shoddy websites and gadgets and apps and conferences. I promise you that any success you might find will be brief. Real traffic will come if you continue to provide real value—every single day. And everything follows from there—big checks, big sponsors, big success.

I call it Elite Retreat, so it has to be elite. In 2009, for our seventh event I decided to raise the price to $8,000. It sold out. *Shocker.* We always sell out because it's not about the price, it's about the value. My company, Elite Retreat, INC, has always been profitable, but only by a slim margin because I invest practically everything back into the product. Currently, we're in the planning stages for our tenth event, which will take place in 2013. You can bet that it will not disappoint, that is, if you can manage to find a ticket.

That's my happy feel-good motivational story for the chapter. Believe in your products, believe in your voice, and keep moving forward, like a badass. But I need to get back to the Coke Theory and tell you a sad story, one in which I learn just how fucking important audience and authority are, after all.

Okay. It's not *that* sad. I just don't make any money because I made the idiotic move to STOP making "coke" and start making "coffee", when everything was going so well with my "coke." okay. I didn't *totally* stop producing all my ShoeMoney stuff; I just stopped totally focusing on it, which is almost the same thing, in my mind.

I got a little distracted by this crazy passion I have for Mixed martial arts and I decided to start a content site called Fighters.com. I was interested, dedicated, and impassioned in the project. I just had no authority building a business in a whole new arena. I never would have gotten the thing off the ground in the first place, never making any money or prospects of money, if I had started it in a natural way. The problem was that I was distracted by all the venture capitalists who were pursuing me at the time, throwing money at any idea I wanted to pimp.

That's two distractions, actually.

Remember, back in the day, I was always the biggest kid in the room. By a lot. So it wasn't like I needed training or anything in order to crush whomever I wanted. As a fat kid, I was constantly trying to prove myself in lots of ways, but physically, I didn't have to. I didn't pick fights because I wasn't out to prove that I had this hidden fighter in me. People could pretty much get that from one quick look at me. I took karate and boxing classes for the pure fun of it.

Side Note: Congratulations to my badass girls who just earned their yellow belts at 4 and 6. Seriously, kiddos, you rock!

Over time, with wrestling in junior high and eventually some Brazilian Jujitsu I got really into the defensive nature of fighting. There's a lot of value in that. In life you can control whether or not you are going to pick a fight, but you never know if someone else is going to come at you. Later in life, I got pretty serious into my training, especially after losing all my weight. I was doing resistance training three times a week and running on the weekends. After six months of that I was in the best shape of my life. Meanwhile, I was really into the UFC and followed all the fighters.

Side Note: Yeah, I know we JUST had a side note like six seconds ago. Deal with it. I have to tell you that if you have never checked out the UFC, you totally must. It's like Fight Club. The rules are there are no rules. Well, there are a few rules. You can't kick in the nuts or use a fish hook, but it's pretty much an open fight and the whole thing takes place in a cage called The Octagon. Seriously, if you need to grow a pair, this is a great thing for you to watch.

Randomly, I knew a lot of the UFC guys already. Some I went to high school with and some I had randomly met later on. Around this time a guy named Matt Hughes was the UFC Welterweight Champion and Tim Sylvia was the Heavy Weight Champion. They both trained in Bettendorf, Iowa at a place called Champions Gym where I saw them on occasion. In 2005, I connected with them and offered to design and host both their websites on my own server, at my own expense because I'm a nice guy. They leaped at the offer and I ended up running both of their websites for quite a while.

At this point, I figured I had some skin in this game already, if not actually my own face. I don't know if it's the same for everyone, but when I get hit in the head it feels like a train is smashing my face into tiny little bits of bone and blood. I found that out in the ring as an adult, pretty much the first time I got hit. The other guy got me smack in the head, really hard and it hurt like a mother fucker. It only took one time for me to decide I wasn't doing that again. I did want to be in the fighting world somehow though, even if I wanted to stay the hell out of the ring.

Enter the venture capitalists.

In the fall of 2007, just after selling Auction Ads, I was getting a ton of visibility. Everything I had my hands in was either booming or selling for large amounts of money. I was a venture capitalist's wet dream: a crazy visionary with no limits. It's not surprising that a bunch of firms were calling me up, fishing around for what was next and how they could get their hands in it, too. I was obsessed with the UFC and my own training at this exact point so I told one investor that my real passion was in this Mixed martial arts website I was developing.

Pretty much, that's all I had to say and he asked me how much he could invest. I randomly threw out the figure of $250K, quickly backpedaling that the figure was for silent ownership of half of the company. I drew up a basic operating agreement, which I'm pretty sure he never even reviewed because it was signed and returned before the end of the week. He wasn't exactly a VC nut-job, just a private investor with a lot of money who wanted to be part of ShoeMoney. Sometimes it's really convenient to have groupies. What can I say? $250,000 was wired into my account on Friday morning and off we went.

On Monday I didn't have a damn clue what to do. I had never run a full company before, and besides the $5,000 loan from J's mom, I had never operated with anyone else's money. Even though the $250K was technically no risk money, I couldn't get into the *what-the-fuck-ever* mindset; maybe it was rooted in the years I lived under the weight of massive credit card debt or something. Even though there was no payback condition on the investment if my venture failed, I was totally wound up. I saw it as my own money. No, actually, it was even heavier than that. With my own money, it's scary, but I know it's on me and I know that I won't fail. But carrying it for someone else was different. I felt tied to it and knew no matter what happened with this new site, I would pay him back from personal funds. That being said, it was nice to know I wasn't alone in the risk. And it was great to have the confidence that someone, pretty much blindly, was happy to fund my crazy idea. He must have known that I have this "I DON'T FUCKING FAIL" thing ticking in me all the time.

We didn't fail for lack of focus or investment, that's for sure.

I bought fighters.com as the domain from a brokerage site and after a series of haggles, actually negotiated a great deal and a sound investment. They listed it at $235,000 and I got it at $60,000. My friends in domain appraisals offered to buy it off me on the spot for $100,000. But I wasn't in this for the quick payout. I wanted to build something I cared about.

The whole thing was backwards to me. Before this point, everything I had ever created came purely from the content. Many times I actually had content before I had any polished idea. But this time I was sitting there with a domain and my thumb up my ass. I had no website and no content to even put on the website that didn't exist. I certainly wasn't going to write it all. That much I knew.

I built the website, really simply, on a Wordpress blog platform that functioned perfectly for what we needed. I built the fighter database by scraping Wikipedia (and another site that actually ended up threatening a lawsuit so I'll leave them out of this) for the stats. Fighters.com really started to come into view when I hired a dozen content writers from across the world to cover every mixed martial arts event, globally. The combined payroll cost me $15K each month.

The writing was engaging. The content was valuable. We started to get significant traffic. By all measurements it was an awesome website. And I couldn't get a single damn advertiser because I didn't know a soul in the industry.

As ShoeMoney I have an audience that exceeds a million and nine years of credibility, which I could (and still can) leverage for any ShoeMoney product or ShoeMoney endorsed product I want. But I didn't have any of that in the world of mixed martial arts. In Internet marketing, I could have a backyard barbeque and get a sponsor for $10,000. Hell, I have worn people's tee shirts at five grand a pop for one day at an industry event. But any time I called anyone for fighters.com they were like, "Who the hell are you, pussy?"

I went through the entire $250K in little less than a year because I couldn't make a cent. I had an awesome website with great traffic but I had disregarded the trust and relationships I had built up as currency within the Internet marketing world while chasing this shiny new prize. It bled me dry, I saw no potential revenues in the sustainable future and I was starting to lose command of everything else I had built. I just wanted out. Right as I was about to about to shut everything down, cut my losses and pay back the investor dude, this random buyer appeared out of nowhere.

Too bad I don't believe in godsends as this is the perfect place to say, "It was a GODSEND!" because I can't think of anything else to call it. I convinced my investor to sell, but in the end he bought me out. To this day I still don't understand that turn of events and what investment he wanted to hold on to with fighters.com. But I got out for a very small percentage of the valuated 50% of $500,000.

I got out and, all things considered, the lessons I learned from the whole painful fighters.com fiasco was worth my investment. I do believe that you learn ten times more from a failure than you do from any success. You can read all day long about what you are supposed to do, how you need to act and react in any hypothetical circumstance, business or otherwise, but until you actually live through that real circumstance, you understand nothing about it.

I actually believe that my ROI on fighters.com was great. I left knowing that under no circumstances should you open a restaurant, just because you like food. I left knowing, without a doubt, that the audience and the colleagues that I have built up are worth more than any monetary value that I could ever imagine or borrow. I left knowing that I am most passionate about my brand and everything that I have rolled up and into this thing called ShoeMoney. And that's the business I want to be in, each new coke at a time.

But sometimes when I look back all I can think is, "*Holy shit.*" Because, for a kid who barely graduated high school, I have done a lot.

Scratch that.

I've done a lot by any standards.

And I'm not even close to being done.

18
Nothing's Changed but My Change

In three words I can sum up everything I've learned about life: it goes on.

-ROBERT FROST

I started with Dickens and I'm ending with Frost, Mo-Fos. I'd say those are some pretty good bookends. Good bookends for sure, not to mention the whole you know, PUBLISHED BOOK THING. How 'bout them apples, Will Hunting? I knew someday my English teacher mom would be proud. So I didn't go to college and get a degree. So what?! I did do a whole lot of other stuff. And that stuff has brought me here, through these stories to a place with something to say.

Something valuable to say.

That's the point, in my opinion. That's why you write a book. So you can leave something valuable behind, something that lasts a little bit longer than a conversation or a blog post. That's why *I* wrote a book, anyhow. Okay, maybe part of it was arrogance—to prove that I could, as a big *"F" You* to the people who said I wouldn't ever do this or amount to much of anything. Maybe another part of it was to make someone, somewhere proud—my wife, my girls, maybe even my mom. Maybe some of that is true. What I know for a fact is that first and foremost I wrote this book for myself.

I wrote it because I can and that makes me proud. Steve Jobs said, "You can't connect the dots looking forward; you can only connect them looking backwards," and I think we can all agree that he was a smart guy. The longer you live and the more life goes on, the truer that becomes. But it is still a real challenge to honestly look at your own life, connect the dots of all the decisions and twists and pull some not-so-gay, not-so-cliché meaning from it all. It takes a lot of focus from a guy with ADD and a lot of strength and confidence even from a guy who has gotten comfortable baring it all every, normal day. ;) That wink is for me.

LOOK MOM! I'M AT WORK!!

It's not just a trophy or a psychology experiment. It's more than that. My book is a testament to what I do, what I've always done and what I will continue to do to find success. And so, my friends and enemies, this book is also for you.

I don't think that's egotistical to say. But my perspective on ego isn't exactly normal, I'll admit. I think it could be egotistical if I was trying to brag the whole time and to talk down to you like a condescending dickhead. But that's not what I do—Ivory Tower or not. I started out as a kid without much prospect. I was fat. I was told I was stupid. I thought a lot of times I was worthless and most of the time I was Ramen Noodle poor. This book isn't about the magic pill I have found, that you can take to make yourself better. The book is about me telling you what I have learned and how I learned those things. Maybe my experiences will you give you a new angle, a new way to get you where you want to be without having to make the same mistakes or going through the same things.

This book is about a lot of things, some of them I will leave for you to interpret .And some of these book's lessons I'm still going to lay out for you in neat little bullet points, all prettied up by my editors. But if you're tired of reading and want to know the big take-away, well, I'm getting there. Don't get your panties in a bundle.

If you were reading this book to figure out how to get-rich overnight, like me, then I'm sorry but I am going to disappoint you because THAT DIDN'T HAPPEN. If you were reading this book to discover the quick fix to a better you, you haven't been listening, ass-face. QUICK FIXES DON'T EXIST. Everything takes time and because of that, our time is really important. Time is all each and every one of us has. How we use our time is what differentiates us all in the end. (If you didn't just underline or highlight that point, you're not getting all the value you could out of this book. I suggest you get off your lazy ass, get a pen or something and go back and underline those last couple of sentences. This is the wrap up chapter alright? Make it useful.)

I'm still riddled with ADD as I'm sure you've noticed. I still have that fat kid living inside me. He probably always will be right there, deep down. I'm still crazy and reckless a lot of the time. I'm still the spitball spitter who struggles with reading comprehension and likes to play video games (just not the persistent world kind). No matter how much time passes and how much I experience, in so many ways I'm still the same kid I always was with all the "issues" I started with thirty-some years ago. I know that now. But over the years I have learned to channel those "issues" and turn them into "advantages" and now I fucking love it.

One of the big points I want to leave you with, probably the nearest thing to a magic bullet that exists is this: **the key to all of the happiness you could ever want and a fulfilling and successful life is taking yourself for who you are.** The earlier you learn to accept yourself, be proud of yourself and let yourself do whatever the hell it is that you're good at, the sooner you'll get IT. And by IT I mean WHATEVER YOU WANT. Getting to the point when you really do live with that kind of self-acceptance is the only thing that really, ever changes. Getting there could take you forever. It could take you thirty years or it could take you until right about now. I'm still the same kid I have always been. I just enjoy being me now. I like being me and I celebrate it with blue toenails and a Ducati. And that is the key to my success.

That's why I like to say that nothing has changed but my change.

I have this deer head that I keep. It's a real, huge, stuffed deer head that I keep, not because I am a hunter or a taxidermist or because we have a weird woodsy décor thing going in my house. I hold on to it because it symbolizes the last day I ever hunted and one of the first days I realized that it's okay to pull your head out of your ass and just be yourself.

The thing was that hunting was the single most important thing to my father. I have never figured out why we're so polar opposite in that area because we're so similar in many other ways. But we differ in our passion (and hatred) for hunting. My dad just wants to sit and hunt all day long waiting for that perfect shot. And if I absolutely have to go out and hunt, well then I want an automatic rifle and a motorcycle that I can drive around until I find something that I can shoot. And when I do find it, I'm going to kill it. Bang. Done. I do not want to sit around all day bored out of my mind. I don't have all day for that shit! I am just not wired for it. I never have been and I never will be. And that's just me.

That didn't matter a whole lot when I was a kid though. If my dad wanted to go hunting it didn't matter that all I wanted to be doing was sitting around playing Nintendo. I had to go.

One morning, really crack-of-the-morning early, when I was about twelve, my dad pulled me out of bed to go deer hunting with him and his buddies. My job was just to sit, very still and quiet, and look out for birds and squirrels. Now, you can't just plop the twelve-year-old me in the middle of the woods with a single 4.10 shotgun and expect me to be quiet. I spent most of the morning blasting birds while my dad and his buddies were off somewhere a half mile away.

Later in the day, I was leaning up against the wall of this dike, fiddling with my gun, kicking stones around, super pissed off about the whole thing. I was bored and tuned out to say the least. Meanwhile, the guys are out driving the deer back towards me. It was completely quiet until, out of nowhere, all the birds flew up from the trees above my head. At the same moment I heard my dad yell, "GEEEEEEEEEEEET READYYYYYYYYYY!!!!" That was followed by a bunch of shots and running. I spun around and before I knew it a HUGE buck went flying over the top my head and then over the dike.

In a panicked state I quickly pointed the gun almost straight into the air and fired off a shot before I even knew what was happening.

The buck kept running.

Shit. I missed.

That's what I thought.

I sort of stumbled up and tried to steady my feet while I reloaded, hoping to get off another shot. All the while I'm thinking, *"Shit I missed. Shit I missed. Shit I missed."*

234

The deer was still running full-on.

In a matter of seconds, the buck went from sixty to zero. He quickly slowed down and in seconds his legs collapsed under his body.

The buck was literally dead in its tracks. That's how it looked from fifty yards away, anyhow. I had to get closer. Maybe the thing could have struggled and reared up and mauled me. But I wasn't thinking about that. I was on automatic. Remember it's only been like 3 and a half seconds since a huge male deer went flying over my head, right? Once I got close enough I could see that it was dead. I had shot it straight through the heart. There was nothing left of the chest but a gaping hole.

I got it.

I was standing right over the deer when my dad and his buddies came jumping over the dike. I will never forget the look on his face as he ran towards me and my kill. It could have been the proudest moment of the happiest day of his life. I got the deer. My dad's son got the deer— right through the heart, for everyone to see.

He knelt down next to the huge buck, pulled out a metal cup and a skinning knife and started gutting. He drained some blood into the cup and handed it to me. And I was like, "Whaaaat?" But he pushed the cup at me while I stood there like an idiot with my head shaking *no, no, no, no.*

My dad didn't budge.

I had to drink the blood.

That's what you do, apparently, with your first deer kill. So I took the cup and in the few minutes that I hesitated, looking down, my dad's idiot friend pulled the cup from my hands and poured the blood all over me. Everyone burst into laughter while I sat there covered in blood, my shock quickly turning to a deep pissiness.

I turned to my dad and said in a low voice, "Fine. Can I be done now? Can I never have to do this again?"

I didn't wait for an answer. I walked towards the trucks and left everyone else behind. I don't care who was happy or proud. I don't care who it disappointed or how. Hunting was not for me. Hunting is very much not for me. I knew that before I was twelve. But at twelve I swore I would never do it again. I would never be so miserable again.

I keep the deer's head as a symbol and a reminder of all of that.

You have to learn to like yourself and keep finding the confidence to be yourself and do whatever it is that you want. That's the start.

Then you need to realize that the people in your life are really important. Not all of them—just the ones that are really with you and who really care about you.

Sometimes it's tough to make that call. I have gotten it wrong once or twice. I made the twenty buck/hour programmer from Auction Ads a millionaire, because I thought it was the right thing to do. I knew it was the right thing to do. Everyone around me told me I was crazy to do so but he had worked really hard for it with me. It felt really good to make him that happy when I could. But I also thought it would incentivize him and drive him to work harder, but instead the money was our rally killer and shortly after we parted ways.

I also have to be careful in choosing who I pimp on my blog. I hold people and products to the same standards that I hold myself to. I have to. It's too easy for marketers to write convincing copy and make tons of promises about a product they know are crap. And then they can make it even harder for people to get a refund and run away with the bank. They'll only get away with it a few times, but that's enough to screw a lot of people and definitely enough to compromise the integrity of my endorsement. You don't have to hawk crap to make money.

My bread and butter is the stuff I sell on my blog. Whenever I sell something, it sells, whether it's mine or someone else's. It's not rocket science and it's no magic secret. It's common sense. I build trust with people and I give them value. That's it. A while back I wrote an eighty-page PDF called the Affiliate Cash Tree. While it was for sale I did not make any income claims or promises of no-work wealth. All that I put up on my blog was a simple description of the product above a purchase button that said "Just Buy My Shit." I had no affiliates publicizing it. My blog was the only place I promoted it. I sold $40,000 worth of product in the first 24 hours. It was a valuable product and people loved it. (And I happily refunded the **two** who were not 100% satisfied.)

These are the ShoeMoney standards I follow for everything I sell:

- I believe that the product/service has real inherent value.
- I know that the product/service is within the scope of my expertise and credibility. There is a purpose for my interest/involvement.
- I differentiate myself from all competition or other vendors and clearly state how and why.
- I transparently show why/how I'm involved or credible to sell product/service and explain how I got started/involved.
- I make it easy for people to contact me. It has never been easier to interact with clientele through email and social media. I embrace this.

You have to establish your credibility. This may take time and lots of active outreach on your behalf. I have credibility because (yup, more bullet points):

- I have sold over $10M+ of other peoples products through email. One guy even bought me a brand new BMW because I sold $500k of his product.
- I was nominated by eBay for a Presidential Award in 2007.
- I had my own segment on Good Morning America, answering questions from small business owners.
- Name the news outlet and I've been quoted or featured in it.

Plus, I'm just a smart, likable guy. What can I say?

That's my business, but my business is also my brand and my name. There's me and there's my brand, with very little space in between. I keep it safe and I defend it when I have to. And you had better believe that I'm careful in choosing who I align myself with these days. No crazy venture capitalists or people looking for a quick buck without something valuable behind it. I'm completely happy and non-threatening unless you mess with me. If you mess with me you can be sure I'll come after you. I'll come after you on my blog, with the full weight of the legal system or even on the street.

Don't forget, I know jujitsu and I have a shit list on a blog that millions of people read. I will stand up and come for you. And if that doesn't work, I will sue you.

Anyone who tells you that it's not worth defending your brand or your reputation hasn't ever done it. Whether it's another person pirating my AdSense check image or the jackass with a bad restaurant deal or any other random douche, people are always telling me that it's not worth it. That I shouldn't waste my time. That I should just focus on doing what it is that I do and rest assured that the bad guys will get it in the end. Well I say, SCREW THAT! Forget karma or odds. I'm the guy that people don't mess with because I won't let you get away with it. I have filed suit in twenty cases and I have never lost. The legal system has never *not* paid off for me, so I'm going to use it.

The problem is that no one cares until they're the ones getting screwed and these bad guys remain unknown assholes who just keep getting away with it while the karma works up. I could have saved so much time and energy and money in this life, already, if anyone took the time to tell me who the bad guys were. That's one of the biggest reasons that I fight. I'm no chicken shit. I stand up for myself, my brand, my family and my friends. I'm still fighting for people even when they've stopped caring. I'll never tell you who you can and can't do business with, but I have a list on my blog of the people I would never do

238

business with ever again. It's an account I keep because I'm looking out for others, too. Use it if you can.

That's not the only reason I care though. The other reason is *Back to the Future*. Remember the Michael J. Fox classics? Maybe the reference is gay or whatever, but I think it gave us a profound truth, which is the biggest reason that I will always stand up for myself and for what I think is right. It all goes back to Biff and McFly. If McFly had just stood up for himself in the first place, there would have been no Biff, no mess, no movie. But it didn't go down the right way the first time. McFly didn't stand up for himself and that affected history. It really fucked his kids.

I think about my girls and I know sure as anything that I won't let them inherit a future like that. I'm in a lawsuit right now with a local guy who ran a bad restaurant deal over me and so I sued him. His kids are the same age as my kids. Who's to say in ten years his kids could look at my kids and think, "We are so much better than them. Dad took Mr. Schoemaker to the woodshed." No. It's not going to go down like that because I'm owning that guy in the public right now and everyone knows what a weasel he is as a result. It's going down the right way the first time. The example I want to set for my kids, without doubt, is that you stand up for yourself.

That's just the kind of guy I am. You can call me super, if you want, but just know that I'm on the lookout for the bad guys. I never let them walk.

Then there are the good people. My colleagues. My groupies. My family. My wife.

No matter how confident and accomplished you are, no matter what degree you hold or how big your bank account is, I don't think you can really be kick-ass all alone. I learned that when I was off chasing shiny objects and a heavyweight presence in the fighting community. I strayed from my audience, my friends, and my people who all come together as a big part of ShoeMoney and without them, I wasn't as good as I could be. I learned that from friends who died too young and from friends who gave me their bed. I learned that from my parents. I have really thrown them over the coals in this book, but I know they did the best they could and they gave me what they could. I learn this every day from my kids. They make me tick, not just with the tones of *"I DON'T FUCKING FAIL"*, they really make me want to be the very best that I can. I learn this from my wife who is my partner, sometimes my accountant, always my best friend and my addiction breaker. Plus, she's hot and she picked me, and that pumps me up every time I think about it.

I have an addictive personality. Yes, this means you can become addicted to me. Just ask my wife. It also means that I become addicted to stuff, easily. Just ask my wife.

Smoking is awesome. I'm not endorsing it or anything. I know it's really bad. Still, I love it. The cigarette I smoked on the way to meeting J for the first time was the last one I smoked—for a very long time. Fast forward to my wedding and I had just one, with my best man, to celebrate. And I loved it. But that was—again—the last one for a long time. And then recently I completely relapsed. It started with one with a drink and then it was two with a drink and then I was a smoker again. Maybe it works like it does with alcoholics. Once an alcoholic, you're an alcoholic whether you're actively drinking or not. So I'm a smoker who recently started up again. It really bothered my wife, which also bothered me. But it wasn't until I realized it was really bothering my daughter, Juliet, that I quit again, cold turkey just like the first time.

I sat her down and said, "Sometimes people make mistakes. Smoking is really bad for you. I started smoking, even though I know it's really bad for me. But now I'm done. I'm done with it."

And I am.

At least for now. ;)

My wife has always been my addiction breaker. I'll say it again. If I had never met her, I'm completely certain I'd be dead. But now it's bigger than just her. Now I have a family too and they're an extension of J and all together, they're my addiction breakers. I want time with my family. I don't want to do anything that takes me away from them, whether that's spending too much time playing a video game or smoking and increasing my chances of dropping dead. My time with my family is too important to me.

My dad's mom was born in 1900. When she was fourteen years old the circus came through her town. Along with the circus came the gypsies. My grandma sat down with one to have her fortune read. The gypsy told her that she would live a long and healthy life, she would have a big family, but she would outlive them all. The prophesy from 1914 all came true, except for my dad's miraculous surgery and the intern who pounded on his chest until his heart started again. Technically he was dead for two minutes at which point everybody else in my grandma's family—her husband and all her other children—were dead, too.

I can't imagine anything worse. I don't want to be the last one standing, outliving everyone I care about and I'm glad that in the end, my grandma didn't have to either. She passed away two months after my dad's heart transplant.

My point here is that the people in my life are important. I don't lose sight of that and I make sure they know it. Money is a good way of proving that.

I realize I pissed away a lot of my parents' money while I was screwing around in college in my cave. A few years ago I did my best to calculate the value of all that pissing away and I came up with ten grand. That year for Christmas I gave them ten grand in a grocery bag. Talk about eyes popping out of heads!!

My wife believed in me, when no one else did and she sacrificed a lot for the life we now have. So after a particularly good year, I paid off the entire balance of all her student loans in one fat check. She was pissed at me for a while because she wanted to own that accomplishment, but eventually she softened since with us now, the money all comes and goes from the same place. She could have paid it off. She would have. But I wanted to do it for her since she's always doing so much for me. (So stop being mad at me already, babe.)

All of these things considered, with all the resources I have now and the community of people I have built around me, I have no equal. I see that all now—looking backwards, connecting the dots.

Five years ago I was on a flight from Lincoln to NYC to ink the deal selling Auction Ads. The guy next to me was a professor from the University of Nebraska who taught in the business school. You know how I feel about classroom learning versus real world knowledge, so I kind of looked down my nose at him like, "Yeah, you're teaching stuff that is out of date and you know nothing. Let me tell you how I just sold this company that generated millions in revenue in only four months." So I told him the story and I figured he would be in awe. But that's not what happened.

Instead he was like, "Wow. It's amazing to me that with all this confidence you wear you didn't have the confidence in yourself to grow your own company."

Then he went back to reading his own stuff.

That set me back a bit.

When you write a book, you have to look back at all the dots. When I look at the dots I can't help but compare myself to my dad because we do have a lot of similarities. And I can't help but wish that he had stayed with Admiral Improvement and kept pushing it forward. I can't help myself from wishing that he had kept making his fishing lures and making more and better products. He had everything he needed. He had the tools and the resources and the audience to keep making more "coke." But he lacked the confidence.

That won't be me. I have already built a ton of stuff I'm proud of, but now I'm building something bigger. I'm taking my brand and flying with it. I know I can do it not only because I have all these people around me, but also because I am such a stubborn mother fucker. When I dig my heels in, I DON'T FUCKING FAIL.

In the end, when you find success, or even a first taste of success, it is fun to flaunt it.

Last year I went back to Moline for my parent's 40th anniversary party. Because my mom was such a popular English teacher, the thing was like a frickin' high school reunion. Tons of kids from back in the day were there, including that one girl, the hottest of the hotties from the class of 1992. She was still looking good and she came up to me.

Very politely she was like, "I hope you don't mind me asking, but what happened to you? You used to be such a mess. You were overweight. You never went to class. You couldn't hold a job. You were VOTED most likely to FAIL. Everyone always felt so bad for your mom because you were such a mess and always in trouble. And now, from what I hear, you're really successful and you look great. So what happened?"

I looked at her, laughed a little and said, "Well, I got laid."

She started laughing too and we talked for a bit. She couldn't help herself from asking how many people I had heard from since becoming successful. Very correctly, she assumed that with the convenience of social media tons of people who wouldn't give me the time of day in high school had started finding me online and hitting me up for some kind of help and advice.

"Yeah," I told her. "That happens a lot."

Finally she was like, "So, what do you say to them when they come calling?"

The same thing.

I always tell them the very same thing.

You should have given fatty a piece.

I'm still the same person that I was way back then. I still dress like I'm 18 in track suits and shit. I still act like I'm 18. I swear when I shouldn't (like in a book) and I don't care. Sometimes it still feels like I'm that fatty and lots of times I still find myself in situations where I'm a little scared. Actually I find that I'm scared shitless a lot of the time, that I'm in a place I haven't been before, just a place I have been training for my whole life.

When I find myself in that place then I know I am where I want to be—a place where I'm pushing myself to be a little better and stronger. I'm always the same me—just a little bit better, every day.

Like I said, it's fun getting to flaunt all my success, especially when no one expected it of me. But that's not why I wrote this book. You don't write a book to prove anything to anyone else. Well, that's not why I wrote a book, at least. You write it to share what you've learned through all the craziness, embarrassments, struggles, and failures which teach us much more than any success ever does. If you're lucky, you have enough success to get people's attention. And then you write a book.

Wait, did I say lucky? If you're lucky? I think you know me better than that by now. I think you know it has very little to do with luck.

That's all I've got to say. That is my life to date. That's how I remember it, anyhow. Well, minus a few details that are definitely too shocking for our first encounter. But after this becomes a New York Times #1 Best Seller and I land a multi-book deal you can trust that I will have more than enough content to keep you coming back. But for now, this is the end. So…

The End.

You're Welcome.

Bonus Material
The Shortcut to Shoeintology

Science is all about finding shortcuts.

–RUDY RUCKER

Surprise.

I'm still here and the value just keeps on a-coming. You can kind of think of this like the bonus material you get when you buy a DVD collection. Isn't that just another reason to prove that movies are better than books? I mean when was the last time that you got bonus material in a book?!?!?

If anyone has ever told you that flipping to the back of the book before you're done is cheating, well congratulations because they're wrong and you're right. Good job on flipping to the back of the book. You now know that there is a bonus chapter that isn't listed in the table of contents AND you're getting to the gist of my stuff faster and more efficiently than all the chumps who are still reading.

What I want to give you here is a kind of like an abstract of my book.

As I've already told you (unless you skipped forward and missed a point I made in chapter one and honestly, that is kind of lazy) this book of mine is the only one I have ever read cover to cover. So I'm sensitive to the fact that you might have some ADD or trouble with reading comprehension. If that's the case, I don't want you to totally miss the big take-aways from my story. In fact, there's this app for people like me (and you) who need abstracts of books and I think it's genius. That being said, I don't want some chimp scanning through my book and giving you the abstract. I want to give it to you myself.

But since this is the only book I've read and now I've read it like, at least, ten times (because my editors kept making me re-read it) I AM NOT READING IT AGAIN. That probably means you're not going to get a neatly ordered list of bullet points that correspond to chapters. I'm just giving you the broad strokes, which I hope came through my stories somewhere in all these chapters. Technically, then, this isn't a true abstract. If you don't like it, well—that's not my problem. You should have read the book cover to cover in the first place. This is the shortcut I'm giving you.

Shoeintology, i.e. How to Think Like ShoeMoney

Think with your mind and not your heart. The dumbest business mistakes I have ever made were because I did them from the heart. I have gone into business with other companies, sold equity in my business for pennies on the dollar, and given lots of cash to colleagues because I was trying to be a hero to people who didn't care. I like my heart. I have a good one. But in business my mind is always the thing to consult.

Don't take advice from anyone who has not done what you are trying to do. You are going to get tons of advice throughout life. The key words you need to listen for when anyone is spouting off are, "Here is what I did in a similar situation." I listen to what everyone has to say but, in my experience (see what I did there), I will take advice from someone who has already been where I am headed. Prioritize that advice above the other 50,000 people who might have good ideas but haven't been where you want to go.

If you see an angle, take it down immediately. I always thought I had a special gift for seeing unique ways to do things. I call them angles. The truth is that lots of people see angles. Very few have the balls to exploit them and almost no one does it fast enough.

30 seconds of awkwardness can pay dividends for life. Don't be shy to ask for a picture with a celebrity. Don't be embarrassed to use everything you have access to for leverage. If you are afraid of looking silly or stupid, you need to have a few near-death experiences and stop taking yourself so seriously. Get what you can and then use what you got.

Don't underestimate what you bring to the table. You are smart. You have an expertise in some area. Whatever you've been doing you've been getting better at it every day. No one sees the world like you do so someone out there will want to "pick your brain." Let them. But set a price. Whatever you know, your time and information are even more valuable if you put a price on it. Business minds have unlimited amounts of money for anything that will give them a positive return on their investment. If you have been successful in an area that someone else needs to know about, why give it away? They will pay; I promise you. My going rate is $10,000 per each 4-hour session. I book that constantly.

(Now, maybe you'll reconsider going back and reading through the book more carefully. Do the math and think about what a deal you've just gotten. I mean, I didn't charge you even close to ten grand for this time, right?)

You never get in trouble for what you do. You always get in trouble for what you say. I bend the lines morally, legally and ethically so I know how it is. I'm no judge. But let me just tell you this much. If you are doing something sketchy, keep your cards close to your chest at all times. Never put into an email or in writing what you can talk about over the phone. Trust no one. I will stop there on this one.

Always stand up for yourself. When I was a kid I never backed down from a fight. As it turned out, I got beat up a lot. But anyone knew that if you came at me you were going to get hit back and I got a lot of licks in, for sure. In business you fight with your mouth and your checkbook. In my business I never back down. I have a "shit list" on my blog at shoemoney.com where I share my experiences in dealings with other people when those people are asses. I do this because most chicken shits never say anything when someone rips them off. I frequently get emails from people thanking me for sharing my experiences with these people or companies. I never tell people not to do business with them. I just share my experience. If someone rips me off, steals from me or causes my family any type of harm I go at them and I take a ton of bricks. These days I have such a reputation that I rarely have to waste my time. I will sue, if you don't back down or right your wrongs. I advise you to do the same.

Surround yourself with people more successful than you. Sure, I have friends that are not ballers, but the majority of people I hang out with are really successful people. Most of them actually have more successful businesses in action than I do. Yes, this means we get to go to the good restaurants together and no one has to worry how we're going to pay the bill. And yes, this means we get invited to all sorts of cool shit. But those are some of the least important reasons. I hang with this type of crowd because of the wealth of experience they have. They inspire me to do better. They also have lots of insight and great experiences they are happy to share. Within that kind of a group I can be like, "I made $3 million in profit last year but now we're stuck on this problem…" They don't flinch at the number. They just get obsessed with fixing whatever issue needs fixing. Most really successful people aren't hoarders with their money or help and I really appreciate that. They also have nothing to gain in bringing you down, so they won't.

Know what your good at and what you are not. I really enjoy programming but the truth is while I can code in about any programming language known to man, I am not very competent with any. So I hire people that are expertly good at it. Also, I can't manage anyone. I just expect people to do what I ask and to know what I mean but that has never worked out for me. So I entrust someone who is a kick-ass manager and everyone is happy. Nobody can be good at everything so this stuff doesn't bother me. Instead I free up my time to do what I'm best at. And in my humble opinion, when it comes to Internet marketing and sales there is no one better than me walking on this planet. So that's what I do and so far, it's working out really, pretty awesome.

Calculate your "work time." I consider work to be anything I do not enjoy doing and I base this idea on the time I spent on salary at the bank. At the time I was earning $70K, which broke down to something like $30 per hour. Now I figure that I get "paid" $30 per hour for things that are work for me like the doing the dishes or the laundry, mowing the yard, or going grocery shopping. If I can pay someone else 1/3 of my "work" rate, I'm totally ahead of the game. Not only do I hate doing those menial jobs, if I'm going to spend an hour "working" it has to be doing something that gives me a positive return. Organizing my life like that has made it a very happy life.

Not to sound like Pollyanna of Mr. Rogers or something, but life can be hopeful. I think my story is inspiring. I think if I have shown anything in this book it's that you don't have to be unhappy or accept being fat. Just because you have ADD or you have trouble in school doesn't mean you're screwed. Just be yourself and remember you're always getting better at something. Your life is really all up to you.

Do what others are willing not to do. If someone made me narrow it down to one piece of advice it would be this. It's the thing I keep coming back to, which in my life has made all the difference. Work harder than someone else is willing to work. Plan Better. Bend the lines legally, morally, and ethically. Take calculated risks. Understand what you can do that others CAN'T or WON'T do—and then do that, too!

Again, you're welcome.

ACKNOWLEDGMENTS

Hmmm…where to start?

There are lots of people I need to thank for making this book a reality as well as for all sorts of life stuff, which happened in order to get me to the point where I wrote the book. Some of you made it into my book by name, and some were just there in spirit, that's just how it worked itself out.

I would like to thank my parents, Joyce and Bob Schoemaker. I know I gave you a lot of grief and sometimes even disappointment. Even though I say that it doesn't matter whether you're proud of me or not, I still can't help it. I do hope I've made you proud. I love you and want you to know that I truly appreciate everything you have done for me.

I would like to thank my mother-in-law, Susan Baron. You not only believed in me but you put your money where your mouth was and helped me to get started. You have continued to support me professionally and personally throughout the years. You are a gem.

I would like to thank my [insert the word that doesn't exist to describe the person who has sacrificed so much of her own self to make my family and business flourish], Anna Zagozda. I really can't thank you enough but let's start with a book acknowledgment. You began as our nanny and have grown into one of the most important people in the company. Thank you for your trust.

I would like to thank my colleague, Justin Handa, for playing a vital role in the ShoeMoney world and showing the same dedication through the best and worst of times.

I would like to thank my business associate, Missy Ward, for all the opportunities and both her professional and personal mentorship over the years.

I would like to thank my friend, Jennifer Slegg, for convincing major conferences to take a risk on the bad boy of the industry and launching my speaking career. But it's more than that. You've been my confident and I cherish our friendship.

I would like to thank my editor, Brienna Pinow, who taught me so much, including proper copywriting (although I don't like to use it).

I would like to thank my writer, Kate Sprouse. Quite simply, the book wouldn't exist without you.

To my friends in the industry—Brian Prince, Greg Hartnett, Stephen Spencer, Neil Patel, Mark Colacioppo, Tigh Buckles, Aaron Wall, Bryan Stevenson, Jon Thompson, Alex Zhardanovsky, Joe Speiser, Mike Sprouse, Chantelle White, David Naylor, Matt Cutts, David Snyder, David Shtief, Jay Wilkinson, Pat Cooper, Danny Sullivan, Brandon Hoffman, Tony Spencer, Andy Beal, Greg & Barbara Boser, Chris Winfield, and Shawn Hogan.

Special thanks to Troy Myerson my attorney, friend and business advisor.

Juliet and Joslyn Schoemaker, every day I feel more useful in your life and look forward to watching you growing into your own. Don't ever forget that you're badasses!

To my wife, Dr. J. Elizabeth Schoemaker, I credit you more than any other person or thing for my personal and professional successes. I love you and look forward to spending the rest of our lives together. Till death do us part. You're bound, even after this book comes out.

AWESOME COMPANIES AND FRIENDS

A week before this week was scheduled to be released I had this epiphany on how I could raise money for charity and also milk some sweet publicity. So I came up with a plan.

Since this book was sure to be a best seller I put out the bat signal to friends and business associates in the industry letting them know I was taking up to 20 companies who can pay $2500 to get their logo and url to their site in my book.

On the first day we filled all the spots. That's right. Tens of thousands of dollars poured in. What a fucking awesome idea.

Just remember who came up with this first cause I am sure TONS of other books are going to steal it and not give me credit.

To all the companies and friends that took part in this - I just want to thank you from the bottom of my heart for your support.

Please visit their sites and see what they are about:

www.safesoftsolutions.com

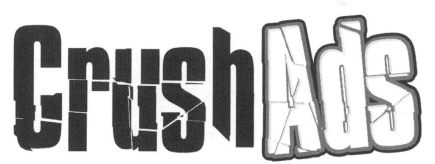

www.conversionvoodoo.com

www.crushads.com

affilaitesummit.com

cre8asite f8rums

cre8asiteforums.com

affiliate.com

a division of Media Breakaway, LLC

affiliate.com

MAXBOUNTY

www.maxbounty.com

GetAds

getads.com

internetmarketingninjas.com

engagebdr.com

seochat.com

www.iacquire.com

www.bannercloud.com

bmielite.com

www.lendingclub.com

www.topvelocity.com

www.anthonymorrison.com

www.johnchow.com

nativerank.com

webmasterworld.com

16664104R00146

Made in the USA
Charleston, SC
04 January 2013